THE
HOLY
CITY
OF
JERUSALEM

The
Holy
City
of
Jerusalem

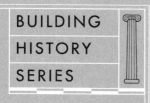

BUILDING
HISTORY
SERIES

THE
HOLY
CITY
OF
JERUSALEM

by Marcia Amidon Lüsted

LUCENT
BOOKS®

THOMSON
━━━━━━✦━━━━━━
™
GALE

Detroit • New York • San Diego • San Francisco
Boston • New Haven, Conn. • Waterville, Maine
London • Munich

Cover: (Clockwise from top) The Dome of the Rock; elderly Jews at the Wailing Wall circa 1880; Entry of Jesus into Jerusalem on donkey fresco 1072.

© 2003 by Lucent Books. Lucent Books is an imprint of The Gale Group, Inc., a division of Thomson Learning, Inc.

Lucent Books® and Thomson Learning™ are trademarks used herein under license.

For more information, contact
Lucent Books
27500 Drake Rd.
Farmington Hills, MI 48331-3535
Or you can visit our Internet site at http://www.gale.com

LIBRARY OF CONGRESS CATALOGING-IN-PUBLICATION DATA

Lüsted, Marcia Amidon.
    The holy city of Jerusalem / by Marcia Amidon Lüsted.
        p.   cm. — (Building history series)
    Summary: Provides an overview of the history of Jerusalem, focusing on some of the city's architecture.
    Includes bibliographical references and index.
    ISBN 1-59018-028-3 (hardback : alk. paper)
    1. Architecture—Jerusalem—Juvenile literature. 2. Jerusalem—Buildings, structures, etc.—Juvenile literature. 3. Jerusalem—History—Juvenile literature.
[1. Jerusalem—History. 2. Jerusalem—Buildings, structures, etc.] I. Title. II. Series.
  NA1478.J4 L87 2003
  720'.95694'42—dc21

            2002007894

Printed in the United States of America

CONTENTS

FOREWORD

Throughout history, as civilizations have evolved and prospered, each has produced unique buildings and architectural styles. Combining the need for both utility and artistic expression, a society's buildings, particularly its large-scale public structures, often reflect the individual character traits that distinguish it from other societies. In a very real sense, then, buildings express a society's values and unique characteristics in tangible form. As scholar Anita Abramovitz comments in her book *People and Spaces*, "Our ways of living and thinking—our habits, needs, fear of enemies, aspirations, materialistic concerns, and religious beliefs—have influenced the kinds of spaces that we build and that later surround and include us."

That specific types and styles of structures constitute an outward expression of the spirit of an individual people or era can be seen in the diverse ways that various societies have built palaces, fortresses, tombs, churches, government buildings, sports arenas, public works, and other such monuments. The ancient Greeks, for instance, were a supremely rational people who originated Western philosophy and science, including the atomic theory and the realization that the earth is a sphere. Their public buildings, epitomized by Athens's magnificent Parthenon temple, were equally rational, emphasizing order, harmony, reason, and above all, restraint.

By contrast, the Romans, who conquered and absorbed the Greek lands, were a highly practical people preoccupied with acquiring and wielding power over others. The Romans greatly admired and readily copied elements of Greek architecture, but modified and adapted them to their own needs. "Roman genius was called into action by the enormous practical needs of a world empire," wrote historian Edith Hamilton. "Rome met them magnificently. Buildings tremendous, indomitable, amphitheaters where eighty thousand could watch a spectacle, baths where three thousand could bathe at the same time."

In medieval Europe, God heavily influenced and motivated the people, and religion permeated all aspects of society, molding people's worldviews and guiding their everyday actions. That spiritual mindset is reflected in the most important medieval structure—the Gothic cathedral—which, in a sense, was a model of heavenly cities. As scholar Anne Fremantle so elegantly phrases it, the cathedrals were "harmonious elevations of stone and glass reaching up to heaven to seek and receive the light [of God]."

Our more secular modern age, in contrast, is driven by the realities of a global economy, advanced technology, and mass communications. Responding to the needs of international trade and the growth of cities housing millions of people, today's builders construct engineering marvels, among them towering skyscrapers of steel and glass, mammoth marine canals, and huge and elaborate rapid transit systems, all of which would have left their ancestors, even the Romans, awestruck.

In examining some of humanity's greatest edifices, Lucent Books' Building History series recognizes this close relationship between a society's historical character and its buildings. Each volume in the series begins with a historical sketch of the people who erected the edifice, exploring their major achievements as well as the beliefs, customs, and societal needs that dictated the variety, functions, and styles of their buildings. A detailed explanation of how the selected structure was conceived, designed, and built, to the extent that this information is known, makes up the majority of the volume.

Each volume in the Lucent Building History series also includes several special features that are useful tools for additional research. A chronology of important dates gives students an overview, at a glance, of the evolution and use of the structure described. Sidebars create a broader context by adding further details on some of the architects, engineers, and construction tools, materials, and methods that made each structure a reality, as well as the social, political, and/or religious leaders and movements that inspired its creation. Useful maps help the reader locate the nations, cities, streets, and individual structures mentioned in the text; and numerous diagrams and pictures illustrate tools and devices that bring to life various stages of construction. Finally, each volume contains two bibliographies, one for student research, the other listing works the author consulted in compiling the book.

Taken as a whole, these volumes, covering diverse ancient and modern structures, constitute not only a valuable research tool, but also a tribute to the human spirit, a fascinating exploration of the dreams, skills, ingenuity, and dogged determination of the great peoples who shaped history.

Important Dates in the Building of the Holy City of Jerusalem

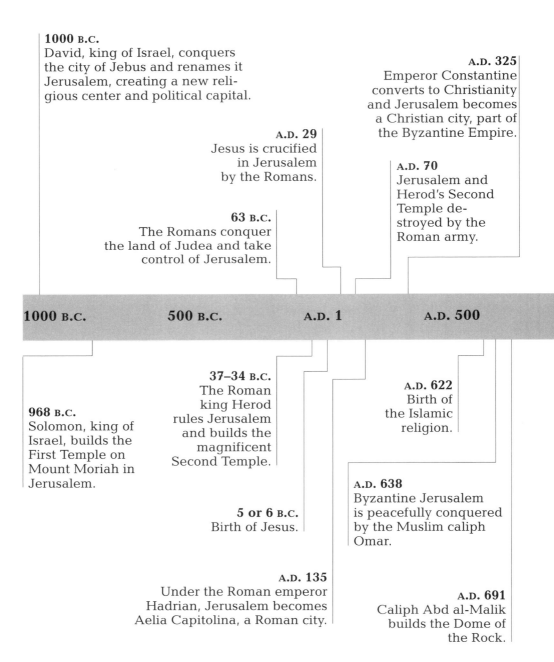

1000 B.C.
David, king of Israel, conquers the city of Jebus and renames it Jerusalem, creating a new religious center and political capital.

A.D. 325
Emperor Constantine converts to Christianity and Jerusalem becomes a Christian city, part of the Byzantine Empire.

A.D. 29
Jesus is crucified in Jerusalem by the Romans.

A.D. 70
Jerusalem and Herod's Second Temple destroyed by the Roman army.

63 B.C.
The Romans conquer the land of Judea and take control of Jerusalem.

1000 B.C.	500 B.C.	A.D. 1	A.D. 500

37–34 B.C.
The Roman king Herod rules Jerusalem and builds the magnificent Second Temple.

A.D. 622
Birth of the Islamic religion.

968 B.C.
Solomon, king of Israel, builds the First Temple on Mount Moriah in Jerusalem.

5 or 6 B.C.
Birth of Jesus.

A.D. 638
Byzantine Jerusalem is peacefully conquered by the Muslim caliph Omar.

A.D. 135
Under the Roman emperor Hadrian, Jerusalem becomes Aelia Capitolina, a Roman city.

A.D. 691
Caliph Abd al-Malik builds the Dome of the Rock.

A.D. 2000
The United States sponsors an Israeli/Palestinian summit at Camp David in Maryland. The Second (Al-Aksa) Intifada sparks more violence.

A.D. 1099
Knights of the First Crusade conquer Jerusalem and massacre most Jews and Muslims.

A.D. 1948
The state of Israel is created, but much of Jerusalem's Old City remains under the control of Muslim Palestinians. The city is divided in half by a wall of barbed wire.

A.D. 1969
The Al-Aksa Mosque altar is destroyed by fire.

A.D. 1538
Suleiman the Magnificent rebuilds the walls of Jerusalem and makes many improvements to the city.

A.D. 1918
Jerusalem falls under the protection of the British after World War I.

1000	1250	1500	1750	2000

A.D. 1187
The Muslim leader Saladin defeats the Christian armies of the Second Crusade.

A.D. 1939–1945
World War II and the Holocaust occur.

A.D. 1967
Israel regains control of Jerusalem after the Six-Day War.

A.D. 1990
First Intifada. A Jewish group places a symbolic cornerstone for a third temple.

A.D. 1995
Prime Minister Yitzhak Rabin officially opens ceremonies marking the three-thousand-year anniversary of the city of Jerusalem.

A.D. 1996
The opening of a new gate in the tunnel running beneath the Temple Mount sparks the Tunnel War.

11

INTRODUCTION

On September 4, 1995, Israeli prime minister Yitzhak Rabin officially opened the ceremonies celebrating the three-thousandth anniversary of the founding of Jerusalem. From 1000 B.C., when King David created his capital city from a small desert village, through the political strife continuing in the Middle East today, Jerusalem, known as the "Golden City," has remained the holiest city in the world, sacred to three different religions.

To understand how Jerusalem evolved from a desert village to what it is today, while enduring periods of great prosperity and total destruction, it is important to know why this city is so important to three different religions and cultures. Each religion has contributed to the building of Jerusalem and the creation of the city as we know it today.

JERUSALEM AND THE JEWISH PEOPLE

The Jewish people believe that King David founded Jerusalem as their religious city, the center of the Jewish faith. David is said to have brought the Ark of the Covenant, a wooden box containing the stone tablets on which were written God's Ten

The modern city of Jerusalem is of central importance to three major world religions.

Commandments, to Jerusalem, establishing it as the City of Peace. Jerusalem is considered to be the center of Jewish religion and culture, and even during those times when Jews were exiled from their holy city, they still considered Jerusalem their promised land, the perfect place for them to live, according to God's word. During those times of exile from Jerusalem into other parts of the world, they would repeat the phrase "Next year in Jerusalem" as a reminder of where the heart of their faith was.

Prime Minister Rabin, in his speech given in Jerusalem in 1995, illustrated the importance of Jerusalem to the Jewish people by saying, "Jerusalem is the celebration of the glory of the Jewish people from the day it was created in the Image of God. She is its heart and the apple of its eye; and our festivities here today are only meant to once again elevate Jerusalem 'above our chiefest joy,' as was the custom of our fathers and forefathers."[1]

JERUSALEM AND THE MUSLIM PEOPLE

Jerusalem is also sacred to the Muslim people, followers of the holy prophet Muhammad, who was born around A.D. 570 in the city of Mecca, located in present-day Saudi Arabia. At a time when Arabs worshiped many gods, Muhammad was impressed by the Jews and the Christians, who worshiped only one god. It is said that Muhammad received a message from God, who gave him the holy teachings of the book of Koran, forming the basis of the religion of Islam. According to the Islamic faith, while he was sleeping in his house in Mecca, Muhammad received a visit from the archangel Gabriel, who instantly brought Muhammad to Jerusalem and seated him on a holy rock, the same rock on which the Jewish king Solomon had built his temple fifteen hundred years earlier. From Jerusalem, Muhammad slowly rose to heaven, where he spoke with Moses and Jesus. Because of this, Jerusalem became one of the holiest cities of the Muslims, and Muslims say that on the final day of the world, God will descend to Jerusalem on black clouds and judge the dead. The rock where Muhammad ascended to heaven is now covered by the Muslim mosque called the Dome of the Rock, whose glittering golden dome is one of Jerusalem's most familiar landmarks. Muslims hold Jerusalem to be the third holiest city in the world to their faith, with only Mecca and Medina

Two Orthodox Jews pass a Palestinian woman in the Muslim quarter of the Old City of Jerusalem.

considered to be holier, and they ferverently protect the site of the Dome of the Rock and the area around it.

JERUSALEM AND THE CHRISTIAN PEOPLE

While the Jewish people believe that the Messiah, who will come to save them from oppression, has not yet come to Earth, the Christian faith believes in the teachings of Jesus Christ, his death, and his resurrection as told in the Bible's New Testament. Christians believe that Jesus was the Messiah, and since he spent his final days on Earth in Jerusalem, it is also one of the holiest cities of the Christian faith. Religious pilgrims, people who journey a long distance to a sacred or holy place, come to Jerusalem to follow in the footsteps of Jesus, to visit the sites of his persecution and death, and to retrace other events of the

Bible. In A.D. 1095, the leader of the Roman Catholic Church, Pope Urban II, instigated the Crusades by urging knights of England and Europe to battle and conquer the city of Jerusalem. He believed that Christians, instead of Muslims, should control such a holy city. This is one example of the many battles fought over Jerusalem by the three religions that hold it to be one of their holiest places. Some of the most famous landmarks of Jerusalem are Christian sites, such as the Church of the Holy Sepulchre, enclosing the place where Jesus died, was laid to rest, and later rose from the dead.

JERUSALEM TODAY

Much of modern Jerusalem is a result of its history of war, destruction, and rebuilding—a cycle that continues into the present day. The city is a unique combination of three thousand years of structures and landscapes built by many different people, religions, and governments. As a city that has experienced almost continual strife throughout its history, every piece of Jerusalem seems to have been built over the remains of an earlier layer of the city. Even contemporary building projects are often halted by the discovery of an archaeologically important site unearthed during construction. This has created a patchwork of historical eras and building methods that make Jerusalem unlike any other city in the world. It also creates a stressful political climate as various religions assert their claims to different areas of Jerusalem, based on a particular era of its history, and none of these issues can ever be easily resolved. By exploring the city during these different eras, it is possible to understand why Jerusalem is one of the most unsettled—and yet most spiritually important—cities in the world.

King Herod's Jerusalem

When the newly appointed Roman ruler of Judea, King Herod, first arrived in the city of Jerusalem in 37 B.C., it was already nearly one thousand years old. Jerusalem had evolved from a mud-brick walled village built near a desert spring to a thriving city surrounded by stone city walls and supplied with water by an underground tunnel system. It was a city that had already been destroyed and rebuilt many times, with its walls breached most recently by Herod's invading Roman army. Its Jewish temple had been ravaged and desecrated. King Herod, however, looked beyond the crumbling city and saw a future capital worthy of glorifying his name and that of the Roman Empire.

KING HEROD'S BUILDING PLAN

Herod's building program in Jerusalem was based on two things: building an impressive city that would be forever associated with him and the Roman republic, and attempting to maintain good relations with the Jewish people who already resented Roman domination and needed to be kept under his control. Many of his improvements were to the structure of the city itself: an aqueduct to carry fresh water from the Bethlehem area southwest of Jerusalem into pools for collecting this water, improved streets, and repaired city walls for protection. Some buildings benefited only the Romans, such as luxurious villas for wealthy families, a hippodrome (a large oval arena where races were held), and an amphitheater for entertainment purposes. Although they are mentioned in ancient accounts of the city, the sites of these constructions have not yet been discovered in modern Jerusalem's archaeology projects. Other structures built

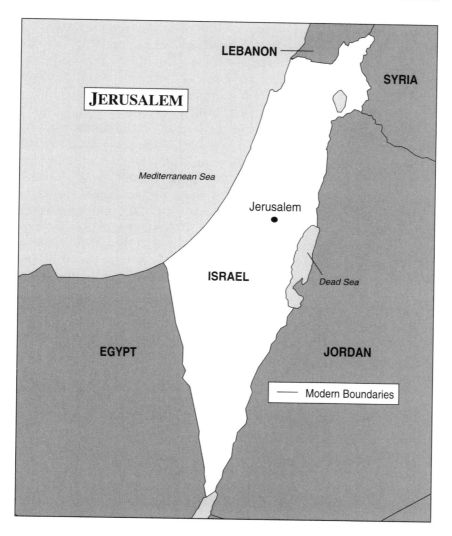

by Herod survive at least in part to this day and are incorporated into many of Jerusalem's most famous landmarks.

HEROD'S PALACE AND THE THREE TOWERS

Herod built an elaborate palace for himself near the modern-day Jaffa Gate in Jerusalem's city wall, complete with three large towers. The palace was built so well that it was used by successive conquerors of Jerusalem up to the present day, and still exists as part of the Citadel of David. The citadel actually had nothing to do with King David, the original founder of

Jerusalem in 1000 B.C. Because the palace was so impressive, people came to believe that it was his fortress, but King David's city of Jerusalem was actually located south of Herod's city. Herod's palace could not have been the king's stronghold, but the name has remained into the present day.

The three towers were each built on a base of huge stones with a decorative outer layer, and each had battlements and turrets and contained apartments and state rooms. These towers were called Phasael (named for Herod's brother), the Hippicus (a friend of Herod's), and the Mariamne (Herod's wife). Of the three, only the base of the Phasael tower remains, near the Jaffa Gate. When the Romans destroyed the palace and the other towers many years later, the base of Phasael was left as evidence that despite the strength of the Jewish city's fortifications, the Romans had overcome them with their superior military powers. The stones are set closely together, trimmed so precisely by stonemasons that they did not need mortar, and each stone is a cube measuring just over four feet on each side. The

These stone arches in the Antonia Fortress date back to the reign of Herod, Roman ruler of Judea from 37 B.C. to 4 B.C.

Phasael tower was originally 135 feet tall, but the remaining base is only 65 feet tall. It has been rebuilt and reused continually since Herod's time. The present top of the tower is actually a minaret, constructed around A.D. 1310 when the tower was used as a mosque.

THE ANTONIA FORTRESS

In the northwest corner of the Temple Mount, a raised area in the center of Jerusalem where the first Jewish temple was built, Herod built the Antonia Fortress to protect and control the temple he would later build. Herod named the fortress for his patron in the city of Rome, Marc Anthony. The Antonia Fortress was built on a rock that stood even higher than the original temple platform, which Herod chose because it would make the fortress difficult to invade. It served as a garrison for Roman troops and later as a defense for Jewish revolutionaries trying to regain control of Jerusalem from the Romans. It was destroyed in a later Roman siege and today only a thirteen-foot-thick section of the south wall can be seen. This section, with several windows, has colored stones actually cemented to the old wall itself, and has been incorporated into a more modern building, which is now used as a boys' school. There are also several sets of sockets that once held massive wooden beams, cut into the stone foundations. The only other trace of Roman construction is a stone arch that is incorporated into a basilica located on the site, and a section of pavement where Jesus is said to have stood when he was brought to the Romans for judgment.

THE SECOND TEMPLE

Herod's crowning achievement in transforming Jerusalem into a fitting capital city was the construction of the Second Temple. Herod believed that his plans for a new temple would not only please the Jews under his control by restoring one of the most important buildings of their faith, but would also result in a magnificent monument that would forever be associated with his name.

The First Temple was constructed in 965 B.C. by King Solomon on the holy site where the biblical Abraham had offered to sacrifice his son Isaac to God, and where King David had brought the Ark of the Covenant to Jerusalem and constructed a temporary shrine. After King David's death the kingdom had grown in population and wealth, and his son, King

KING HEROD, MURDERER AND MADMAN?

King Herod is remembered for his impressive building projects, both in the city of Jerusalem and places such as the mountain fortress of Masada, the port city of Caesarea, with an amazing artificial harbor, and Herodium, his palace and mausoleum. He is also remembered, however, for his cruelty, explosive temper, and ruthless dealings with anyone who opposed his government.

During his reign he executed or arranged to have murdered his wife, Mariamne, his popular brother-in-law, his mother-in-law, his two sons by Mariamne, and his oldest son by another wife. When Herod came to power in Jerusalem, he executed more than half the members of the Sanhedrin, the supreme religious and civic council of the Jews. He cruelly suppressed any signs of rebellion among his subjects and always had Roman legionnaires (soldiers) standing by to carry out his orders.

Toward the end of his life, Herod became afflicted with a mysterious disease whose symptoms included uncontrollable itching, fever, coughing, worms, and increasing madness. Although he had his wife Mariamne killed, he still loved her and would awaken screaming her name. During this stage of his life, Herod is said to have ordered the famous biblical Massacre of the Innocents, when he ordered every male infant in the area killed in case one should be the foretold king of the Jews (Jesus) who would usurp his power.

Herod was approximately sixty-nine years old when he died of a fever. He was old and alone, having either killed or alienated all those close to him.

Solomon, constructed a magnificent temple where his father's smaller temple had stood on Mount Moriah, a high hill above the city. Referred to as the First Temple, Solomon's temple was said to have had cedar beams, bronze pillars, ivory doors, and many gold and stone ornaments, and the Ark of the Covenant was contained within the inner chamber, called the "Holiest of Holies." The First Temple was destroyed when a group of people called the Chaldeans of Babylon laid waste to the city of Jerusalem in 597 B.C. and banished the Jews. In 515 B.C., when the Jews returned to Jerusalem, Zerubbabel, the governor under the rule of the Persians, rebuilt the temple, but it was not as large or as beautiful as the original building. By Herod's time, it was suffering from neglect and was far too small for the numbers of worshipers who came there. Herod decided to renovate and expand this Second Temple. Although he was bound by specific biblical instructions that prohibited changing the size or shape of the sanctuary, Herod was able to make the building itself more beautiful and expand the area around it.

PREPARING FOR THE CONSTRUCTION OF THE SECOND TEMPLE

Herod's Second Temple took more than eighty years to complete. Although Herod had many fine architects at his disposal, he acted as his own architect in constructing this masterpiece. The first step in creating a temple as magnificent as he envisioned was to enlarge the area on the Temple Mount, as Jerusalem's Mount Moriah had come to be called. Herod filled in part of the Typopoean Valley to the west of the mount, as well as a depression to the north, and constructed a series of vaulted arches along the southern slope of the hill. This created a

The enormous Temple of Herod dominated Jerusalem's landscape at the time of the Crucifixion.

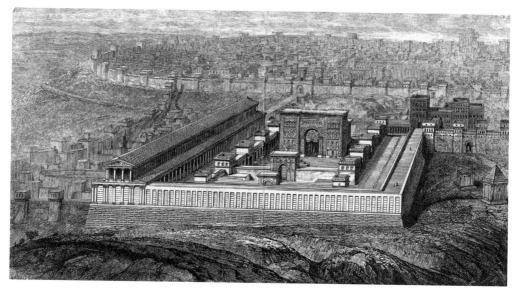

rectangle much larger than the original temple's area. From there, Herod's workers dug down to the bedrock, fifty to sixty feet below the surface, and started the first row, or master course, of stones for what would be the temple's retaining wall. This course was made sixteen feet thick to support the tremendous weight of the temple complex that would be built above it. In order to build additional layers of stone without having to hoist enormous blocks into position, the workers would fill the area behind the new stone retaining wall with earth until the level was equal to the newly laid stones. Thus the next layer would be built from above, rather than lifting the stones from below.

The first courses of stone in this huge retaining wall that would surround the entire Temple Mount were ashlar stones, squared building stones that were quarried and then shaped and chiseled so smoothly that mortar was not needed to keep them in place. Some of these stones in the master course have been investigated by archaeologists and found to be as much as forty feet long, ten feet high, and fourteen feet thick, weighing as much as five hundred tons. A single stone of this dimension would be bigger than any of the stones at Stonehenge, in England.

BUILDING WITH STONE

The primary stone used for building in Jerusalem was limestone. According to geologists, the Holy Land was once at the bottom of an ancient sea. The skeletons and shells of microscopic sea animals sank to the ocean floor, and over the millennia were compressed by the layers of sediment above them until they formed white limestone. When the movement of the earth forced this ancient sea floor up above sea level, it formed mountains of limestone. With the passage of time, wind, water, and volcanic action eroded this material, forming soil and exposing the rock.

Jerusalem's location between the sea and the desert provided it with a rich geological mixture: granite bedrock covered by various types of colored limestone and chalk, as well as some sandstone east of the city. Limestone was a nearly perfect material for building. It was plentiful, as well as being soft and easy to quarry, and after being exposed to the environment it would harden. In the earliest days, limestone could be quarried by hammering or drilling several holes into the rock in a straight line and then driving wooden pegs into the holes. When these pegs were soaked with water, they would expand, exerting pressure on the rock until it split in a fairly straight line. Then masons would shape the rough surfaces or faces of the stone using adzes (an axlike tool with a curved chisel-like head) and chisels.

By King Herod's time, and with the expertise of the Roman builders, limestone could be quarried in underground caves with chisels and saws and cut into blocks that were approximately the correct size. These quarries were often located uphill from the temple building site, making it easier to transport the blocks of stone by rolling them downhill on wooden rollers. On a hilltop near the northwestern corner of Jerusalem's Old City, there is an area that was extensively quarried by Herod for his temple, since it is 125 feet higher than the Temple Mount and the huge stones quarried there could easily be moved downhill. A fifty-foot-long stone column still attached to the bedrock that it was being carved from can still be seen here today. Apparently the workmen noticed a defect in the stone that made it unsuitable, and abandoned it, half-quarried, where it lay. The dimensions of the column are similar to those described in the construction of Herod's temple by the ancient historian Josephus.

Because of the extensive quarrying necessary to supply enough stone to build the huge temple, the ground beneath Jerusalem is riddled with caves and passages, and much of the city's original terrain has been changed as higher areas were carved away. The area beneath the Temple Mount itself was also quarried, and as a result, has many chambers with stone pillars that supported the temple above and could have been used for storage. One of these chambers, with eighty-eight stone supports, was misnamed Solomon's Stables by the crusaders of the twelfth century, and they used it to stable their own horses and camels. Muslims currently use this space as a mosque.

THE TEMPLE WALLS ARE CONSTRUCTED

Once the bottom course was laid and the temple enclosure was defined, the retaining walls soon began to rise. Each stone was trimmed and fitted so tightly that even without mortar a knife blade or a piece of paper could not be wedged deeply between them. Each course of stone was set back approximately an inch

HEZEKIAH'S TUNNEL

One of the oldest constructions still existing in Jerusalem today is Hezekiah's Tunnel. Although Jerusalem is now a modern city with a sophisticated water system, even in the centuries before the birth of Christ its water supply was being protected and upgraded. Hezekiah, who was king of Jerusalem from 727 to 698 B.C., realized that King Solomon's original tunnel from the water spring of Gihon, outside the city walls, into Jerusalem, was a dangerous weakness. Attackers could enter the city through this water tunnel or block the supply and make Jerusalem vulnerable. Hezekiah ordered another tunnel built that would connect the springs and the Pool of Siloam inside Jerusalem without being visible to potential attackers.

Hezekiah's Tunnel is more than sixteen hundred feet long and shaped like a huge letter *S,* suggesting that the workers who carved it were following a natural crack in the rock where water already trickled. This would also explain how they managed to have fresh air to breathe while working by the light of oil lamps, which use up oxygen. Two gangs of workmen tunneled toward each other from either side of the Hill of Ophel, and halfway through they began to hear each other's progress. In the *Oxford Archaeological Guides: The Holy Land*, author Jerome Murphy-O'Connor translates the inscription the workers carved into the tunnel wall where they met:

> Behold the tunnel. This is the story of its cutting. While the miners swung their picks, one towards the other, and when there remained only 3 cubits to cut, the voices of one calling his fellow was heard—for there was a resonance in the rock coming from both north and south. So the day they broke through the miners struck, one against the other, pick against pick, and the water flowed from the spring towards the pool, 1200 cubits. The height of the rock above the head of the miners was 100 cubits.

This inscription in the rock, called the Siloam Inscription, was actually chiseled out of the wall by vandals in the early 1900s, but was recovered and sent to Constantinople. Israel is hoping to have the inscription lent to Jerusalem where it can be seen as part of an exhibit in the Israel Museum.

The miners did not manage to meet exactly, but the spot where they met is only two inches out of alignment. In places where the rock was difficult to cut, the ceiling of the tunnel is barely above a person's head. The water still flows today and the tunnel can be walked through.

from the row beneath it, giving the wall a slightly pyramid-like appearance. The walls towered as much as one hundred feet above street level.

Once finished, the Temple Mount area covered forty acres, or 172,000 square yards. Crowning this platform was the temple, which was built of white limestone trimmed in gold. In his book *Jerusalem: A History of Forty Centuries*, Teddy Kollek writes:

> The ground-plan and interior arrangements of the Temple proper . . . could not be altered [according to biblical specifications]. But Herod doubled its height and vastly amplified the porch, so that the building seemed to soar. This impression was heightened by its being set atop a series of descending terraces with huge courts, colonnaded and walled. The Temple was built of large blocks of white stone, its façade plated with gold, so that at a distance it appeared like a mountain covered with snow.[2]

These gates lead to an underground support structure known to the crusader Christians as Solomon's Stables, one of many chambers beneath the Temple Mount.

THE WESTERN WALL

Although Herod's beautiful temple was later destroyed, a small part of it is still visible today. Of all the landmarks in Jerusalem that can be traced back to King Herod, a portion of the temple's retaining wall called the Western Wall is the most famous. Often called the Wailing Wall, it is one of the holiest places for Jews because it is as close as Jews can come to the site of the Jewish temples that once stood on the Temple Mount. Traces of Herod's original temple construction can be seen in this wall and in the remnants of a huge arch that once supported a bridge from the city's street to the temple, and in another arch that once held a huge staircase from street level to the temple's platform.

The Agency for Jewish Education website offers an excellent description of the Western Wall, also called the Kotel:

> Above ground, the Kotel has 24 rows/layers of stones of different dressing (chiseling and shaping) and decreasing in size and age. Excavations in 1867 revealed that nineteen more rows lay buried underground which reach down to a paved road which ran along the foot of the wall. Underneath this paved road are another nine layers which constituted the foundations of the wall and which have never been uncovered. In 1968 the ground in front of the Kotel was excavated to reveal two of the buried rows of stones. Above ground there are seven layers of huge Herodian stones from the Second Temple era. They are dressed at the edges only. Above these are four layers of smaller, plainly dressed stones from the Roman or Byzantine periods. The upper stones were constructed from the Arab period (seventh century) onward. The small stones in the upper section of the wall were added by Sir Moses Montefiore [in 1866] in an attempt to repair the wall. However, it is not easy to distinguish exactly who added what to the original wall as a similar style of construction was used over many centuries.[3]

The road uncovered during this excavation was roughly forty feet wide and paved with huge stone slabs. In Herod's time, it was the main north-south thoroughfare in Jerusalem.

Thousands of years later, much of this area was covered by an Arab neighborhood built against the Western Wall during the division of the city into Arab and Jewish sections. It was not un-

Crowds of Jews gather along the Western Wall for prayer and remembrance.

til the Jews regained access to the Old City that archaeologists were able to study the Western Wall area.

In 1967, after the Arab Israeli Six-Day War in Jerusalem, the slum that occupied the section of the city next to the Western Wall was torn down:

> The war ended on Saturday, June 10. That night the bulldozers of the combat engineers entered the Old City. Twenty trucks waited . . . to evacuate the Arab families of the . . . warren of tumbledown buildings that surrounded the Western Wall courtyard. The bulldozers worked all night. By morning, they'd carved a wide field in front of the Wall and lengthened the exposed stretch of Herodian stones to 200 feet.[4]

The entire area was cleared and converted into a large paved open space. This was partitioned off into one section for women and another for men, making it a place of pilgrimage and prayer for all Jews (in Judaism, men and women separate to pray so they are not distracted by the opposite sex). Jewish people gather there from all over the world to pray and leave slips of paper with prayers written on them between the stones of the wall.

The Western Wall illustrates, perhaps better than any other place in Jerusalem, how the city has been created in layers according to the different cycles of building and destruction it has endured. A visitor standing at the wall can view the stones placed through the centuries—from King Herod's time to those added to the wall only a few hundred years ago—illustrating the entire spectrum of Jerusalem's history. This makes the Western Wall truly fitting as one of Jerusalem's most famous images. As Rabbi A.I. Kook, former chief rabbi of Israel, once said about the Wailing Wall, "There are men with hearts of stone and there are stones with human hearts."[5] To those of the Jewish faith, the wall represents the struggles and losses of their history and has become almost a living symbol of their beliefs.

THE DESTRUCTION OF HEROD'S JERUSALEM

Jerusalem's glory as King Herod's capital city lasted only until the Romans once again besieged the city after a Jewish revolt in A.D. 70. His beautiful temple was enjoyed in its completed form for only ten years before it was totally destroyed, but many of his most magnificent buildings remain, at least in part, in the Western Temple Wall, the Citadel of David, the Phasael Tower base, and other locations that are continually coming to light in archaeological excavations around the city. The destruction of Herod's Jerusalem gave way to the construction of a truly Roman city and the next phase of Jerusalem's history.

ROMAN JERUSALEM

After many years of Roman rule under Herod and his successors, the Jews finally revolted against Rome in A.D. 70. They managed to successfully attack the Roman garrison in Jerusalem and even defeated the Romans' Twelfth Legion as it marched toward the city to put down the uprising. Once the Jews were safely behind the walls of Jerusalem, it took a siege by Roman emperor Titus and his Tenth Legion to defeat them and regain control of Jerusalem for the Romans.

THE DESTRUCTION OF HEROD'S JERUSALEM

The Jewish people had the advantage of being thoroughly familiar with the terrain around their city, but the Romans had the use of their heavy war machinery. They had huge swinging battering rams, heavy catapults, and rapid-fire dart throwers. They also constructed tall assault towers that could be rolled up to the city's walls. These towers were tall enough to allow Roman archers to fire on Jewish defenders, especially those on the walls firing down on the Romans who were using battering rams to break down the walls at ground level. Wooden shields covered with animal hides protected the structure of the assault towers from the arrows and burning oil that the Jewish fighters launched from the top of the walls.

Roman war machinery required wood for building it. Josephus, the Roman historian, writes of the effect that the Romans' demand for wood had on the countryside surrounding Jerusalem:

> The Romans . . . had cut down all the trees that were in the country that adjoined to the city. . . . And truly, the

very view itself of the country was a melancholy thing;
for those places which were before adorned with trees
and pleasant gardens were now become a desolate
country every way, and its trees were all cut down: nor
could any foreigner that had formerly seen Judea and
the most beautiful suburbs of the city, and now saw it
as a desert, but lament and mourn sadly at so great
a change.[6]

The Jews, however, held out against the Roman war machines for longer than it would have seemed possible. After sev-
enteen days of continuous battle, the Romans had an assault
tower and battering rams in place at the wall near the Antonia
Tower. The Jews tunneled under these machines from within
the city, supporting their tunnel with wooden props that had
been covered in flammable material. When the rams were
moved into position and began to batter the wall, the Jews set
fire to the wooden supports. As the wood burned away, the supports crumbled and the tunnel fell inward, taking with it the

*Jerusalem was reduced to ash by Roman legions after the Jews revolted against Roman
rule in A.D. 70.*

Roman battering rams and assault tower and putting an end to the Roman assault of the Antonia Fortress.

Eventually, however, the Roman legions succeeded in breaking through the walls and taking Jerusalem. As the battle raged and the city and its inhabitants fell to the Romans, the greatest casualty was Herod's magnificent Second Temple.

The Romans marched into the city and onto the Temple Mount, and many of the Jews fled into the temple. Everything of value in the temple was looted and many sacred objects were later paraded through the city of Rome in a celebration of the victory. The Roman soldiers set fire to the temple, hoping to find the gold and silver that were rumored to still be hidden within. Many of the Jews who took refuge in the temple were trapped in the flames. The historian Josephus gives us an eyewitness view of the temple's destruction:

> The flame was also carried a long way, and made an echo, together with the groans of those that were slain; and because this hill was high, and the works at the temple were very great, one would have thought the whole city had been on fire. Nor can one imagine anything either greater or more terrible than this noise.[7]

Josephus also recorded a legend that was told about the temple's destruction. As smoke and flames engulfed the roof, one of the temple's priests was said to have climbed to the top of the main tower. Holding the keys to the temple's sanctuary, he cried, "If you, Lord, no longer judge us to be worthy to administer Your house, take back the key until You deem us worthy again."[8] According to the legend, a hand appeared from heaven and took the key from the priest.

After the temple had stopped burning, the Roman soldiers pried apart the stones with long bars to retrieve the melted gold and silver, leaving no two stones standing on another. Many of the temple stones were pushed over the edge of the Temple Mount into the valley below, and recent explorers and excavators have uncovered these large stones and other debris cast down by the Romans from the temple's walls. They toppled columns and arches and knocked down upper walls, and the fragments still litter the paved street below the Temple Mount, which has been unearthed and studied by archaeologists. The Romans even chiseled away at the foundations of the huge

The Second Temple, the jewel of ancient Jerusalem, was destroyed by fire during the Roman invasion.

retaining wall, and much of it was also destroyed except for the small portion that became the Western Wall. It is even written that the Romans plowed under all the ruins of Jerusalem and that the ground was strewn with salt to prevent anything from growing there. Jerusalem was totally destroyed. None of its walls escaped ruin, and only Herod's palace and his three towers still stood, as evidence to the world that all the strength of Jerusalem had been no match for the might of Rome.

THE END OF JERUSALEM

The Romans destroyed not only the city of Jerusalem but most of its inhabitants as well. The city had already been suffering from famine since the invading Romans prevented the Jews from leaving the city to find food, which killed many of them. Those who slipped out of the city to forage for food were often captured and crucified in grotesque positions by the Romans. The number of people killed each day was so great that there was no room left on the city walls for any more of their crosses. It is also said that when the Arab mercenaries (hired soldiers) of the Romans discovered that many inhabitants were hiding their gold coins by swallowing them, they slit open the stomachs of thousands in a single night. Jews who managed to survive were taken as Roman slaves, sometimes dying in the coliseums as part of the Roman gladiator entertainments. The rest of the Jews fled from Jerusalem and took refuge in other cities in the area, and Jerusalem was now off-limits to anyone of the Jewish faith. Emperor Titus built a camp on a remaining portion of the city to house the legion of Roman soldiers who would keep watch over the ruined city, and Jerusalem ceased to exist.

A NEW ROMAN CITY

The site of the destroyed Jerusalem was now a clean slate for the Romans to build upon. There was an abundant supply of building materials in the ruins of Jerusalem's structures. Many of the stone blocks quarried in King Herod's time, identifiable because of the specific way in which they were carved, can be found in later structures of the Roman period, making it difficult for modern archaeologists to precisely date many structures. This reuse of scavenged building materials is called architectural cannibalism, when inhabitants of an area strip ancient monuments of materials (such as the limestone facing that once covered the pyramids in Egypt) for use in newer public buildings or even houses. Blocks of marble and limestone were even burned in kilns to extract the lime from the stone for other purposes.

The first new structures built by the Romans after A.D. 70 were simply for the construction of a military camp for the occupying Roman legion. Roman camps were built according to a similar plan no matter where in the world they were located so that the soldiers would feel securely oriented anywhere. This military camp was called a *castrum*, and was roughly rectangular in shape. It would have two main streets running north to south and east to west, and where they crossed there would be a large open space called a forum where the soldiers would gather daily to receive orders. Initially, soldiers would live in tents pitched in rows, which would often be replaced by wooden shelters later.

In Jerusalem, the Romans' Tenth Legion erected a camp southwest of the Temple Mount. There were already two Roman streets in place, the Cardo Maximus and a secondary Cardo, which met outside the camp near what is now the Damascus Gate. The camp had its own temples, baths, and other public structures to serve the soldiers' needs.

AELIA CAPITOLINA

From A.D. 130 to 131, the new Roman emperor, Hadrian, journeyed to the eastern part of the Roman Empire. At this time, he decreed that a new Roman colony be constructed over the remains of Jerusalem, to be named Aelia Capitolina. He named the city in part after himself, since his whole name was Publius Aelius Hadrianus, and partly in honor of the god Capitoline Jupiter, to whom he built a shrine on the Temple Mount. This replaced the Roman military camp with an actual city, which was built in the Roman architectural style and followed the same plan as most of their other colonial cities.

One of the first structures built in Aelia Capitolina still survives today, but only because later structures were built above it and unwittingly preserved it. Beneath the present-day Damascus Gate, which was built in the 1500s, excavators have found a second-century Roman gate that is nearly intact. This was the northern gate of Aelia Capitolina, although it stood alone as a triumphal arch or symbol of Roman domination since the city was not completely enclosed by walls at the time of its construction. In later years, when Jerusalem was once again walled, the Roman gate was incorporated into the system of walls built there. This Roman gate had three entrances that were protected by massive towers, and each entrance was an arch decorated by columns on high bases. The walls of this tower were built with stones that most likely came from the ruined retaining walls of the Second Temple, since the carved margins of the stones are typical of King Herod's buildings. The eastern tower of this Roman gate has survived to a height of approximately forty feet (twelve meters), almost its original height, and the western tower is nearly thirty-six feet (eleven meters) high, each with a flight of steps that gives access to the roof of the towers.

New excavations conducted from 1979 to 1984 uncovered most of this Roman gate below the Damascus Gate. Visitors can now descend to the old gate's level and walk through it, or climb

A view of the sixteenth-century Damascus Gate, beneath which a nearly intact second-century Roman gate was discovered.

the stairs inside the towers. Above the eastern entrance to the gate is an inscription fragment in Roman Latin that ends "by the decree of the decurions of Aelia Capitolina,"[9] proving that the gate dates from the time of the new Roman city.

There was another triumphal gate on the eastern side of the city, erected at the same time. All that remains of this gate is an arch called the Ecco Homo (meaning "Behold the man," referring to the biblical words the Roman prefect Pontius Pilate said about Jesus when presenting him to the crowd at his judgment) arch, incorporated into the Ecco Homo basilica because it was mistakenly thought to be the arch under which Jesus was judged by the Romans before his death.

BUILDING THE ROMAN CITY

Once Hadrian decreed that a new colonial city was to be built, it was laid out and constructed according to the typical Roman city plan. Roman camps and towns in outlying territories were meant to demonstrate the glory of Rome, concentrating Roman culture and civilization and enticing the native peoples to adapt to Roman ways. Aelia Capitolina was built in the classic Roman pattern, in the shape of a square, and much of this design is still

THE TIME OF JESUS

One of the reasons why Jerusalem is such a holy place for the Christians of the world is that Jesus Christ, known to Christians as the Messiah and the Son of God, spent the last week of his life in the city and was crucified there by the Romans in approximately A.D. 29. Jesus and his followers came into Jerusalem at a time when it was a Roman province, heavily policed by Roman soldiers who put down any attempts at a Jewish revolt.

Jerusalem was ruled at this time by Pontius Pilate, a Roman prefect who was said to be determined to subdue the Jewish people rather than cooperate with them, as others had done in the past. Jesus entered Jerusalem to the cheers of the crowds, but he alienated the traders at the temple by overturning their stalls and telling them they had no place in the House of God. Eventually Jesus was arrested by the Romans and condemned to death.

As was usual at the time, Jesus was crucified on a wooden cross, a traditional Roman method of execution usually used for slaves and rebels. The condemned man was forced to carry a heavy wooden crosspiece to his place of execution, where his arms would be tied or nailed to this horizontal crossbar and his feet nailed to the upright post that the crosspiece was nailed to. Jesus would have died of suffocation as the pressure on his arms and chest slowly squeezed and closed his breathing passage.

After his death, Jesus' body was taken to a tomb carved into the rock at a site called Golgotha, or "the Place of Skulls." This was a popular area to cut tombs since the rock there was faulty and not suitable for quarrying and building. After three days, Jesus rose from the dead and ascended to heaven, according to the Bible. He did appear to his disciples, and they and a few others, numbering only 120 people at most, were the basis for the first Christian church. These people were at first called Judeo-Christians, since they followed Jewish law while awaiting the return of Jesus, the risen Christ or Messiah for whom the Jews were waiting. Eventually, as they were persecuted by other traditional Jews, the Christians would become completely gentile, or non-Jewish, especially after the destruction of Jerusalem in A.D. 70 after which all Jews were banned from the city.

evident today in modern Jerusalem's Old City. It was the Roman city design that left a lasting mark on Jerusalem's present layout by creating the four quarters of the Old City.

The Romans were master builders and used many sophisticated materials and techniques. Not only did they construct their buildings with local stone—either quarried or reused from destroyed buildings nearby—but they also used bricks, clay, and concrete. The bricks were made from clay, with straw or other fibrous material added for strength, that was shaped in wooden molds and dried in the sun. Many of the bricks made by Roman soldiers were stamped with the individual symbol of their legion, a boar. The Romans had discovered how to make cement by heating a soft, claylike type of limestone, which could then be mixed with sand, water, and crushed stone or gravel to create concrete. Concrete was used for lining the stone passages of aqueducts to make them watertight.

The first constructions necessary to the new city of Aelia Capitolina were roads and streets. There was a new road constructed from the city to Caesarea, a Roman coastal city, terminating at the same Roman gate now located beneath the Damascus Gate. From here, one entered the city on the Cardo.

THE CARDO

Although many roads in Roman provinces were made of crushed rock or were merely dirt footpaths, the Cardo built in Aelia Capitolina was made of pavement stones. Ditches were dug on both sides of the intended street and lined with curbstones, and then the area between them was dug even deeper and filled with layers of varying sizes. The top layer would be the actual pavement of the road, rising slightly in the middle of the road to force water to the sides. There were gutters on both edges of the road where rainwater could drain from the street into underground sewers. The Cardo extended 3,117 feet, or six-tenths of a mile, from the Damascus Gate to Mount Zion, but to create the straight level street that the Roman engineers wanted, they had to alter some of the city's hilly terrain. On the southern side of the street, they had to lower the ground level by cutting into the rock; on the northern side, they had to fill in low areas to raise the ground level. This engineering practice is called cut and fill, and is still used today to build roads in hilly terrain. The resulting Cardo was seventy-five feet (twenty-three meters)

A row of columns runs parallel to the reconstructed Cardo, the main road of Byzantine and Roman Jerusalem.

wide and lined with parallel rows of columns. The columns created a sidewalk shopping area removed from the traffic of the street. In later eras, some sections of the colonnaded Cardo were completely vaulted and roofed to create an indoor shopping area.

In certain areas of the street, there were sets of stepping-stones imbedded in the pavement to allow pedestrians to cross the street without stepping in water, mud, and other trash. These stepping-stones were spaced to allow the wheels of carts and wagons to straddle them, and in many ancient Roman city streets the ruts of this wheeled traffic are still visible, worn into the paving stones. The stepping-stones also forced wheeled traffic to slow down on streets that were busy with pedestrians.

Jerusalem's Cardo remains in part today and is once again being used as a shopping area. After the Six-Day War, when the Jewish Quarter was being restored, part of the Cardo was discovered and repaired. While some of the columns can still be seen at nearly their original height, others are only evident as stumps several feet high, used to support streetlamps or even as chopping blocks in butcher shops.

THE ROMAN CITY CENTER

The next Roman structure that was integral to life in a Roman city was the forum. This was an open space, usually a square, where business would be conducted, markets were often held, and state affairs were decided in a nearby basilica, a word which in Roman times referred to a government building and covered marketplace (rather than a religious structure as it connotes now). Forums were usually located where the two major streets of the city—the Cardo and the Decumanus—crossed, but given the geography of Aelia Capitolina and the more unusual arrangement of the streets, there were actually two forums. One was located near the Antonia Fortress, and the other at the site of today's Church of the Holy Sepulchre. In places where sections of the original Roman pavement still exist, there are Roman game boards carved into the stone, where soldiers passed their time playing dice games while on duty.

THE WATER SUPPLY

Aelia Capitolina was supplied with water by a system of aqueducts, many of them built in King Herod's time. Roman aqueducts were meant to transport water by gravity alone, without the use of pumps, and they were gradually graded from high areas to lower elevations. The water ran in a covered conduit made of stone and lined with waterproof cement. This channel was usually only half full of water, leaving ample space to make allowances for deposits of calcium carbonate that would eventually narrow or clog the water passage. Aelia Capitolina's water came from the Pools of Solomon above the town of Bethlehem, southeast of Jerusalem, and was carried by an aqueduct supported on stone arches until it reached the city where it was either distributed by pipes or collected in several large pools. Elevating the aqueduct prevented the water from being stolen or poisoned, and helped to maintain the necessary grade to keep the water running toward the city. The change in elevation from the pools to Jerusalem kept the water moving under pressure without the need to use pumps once it reached the city.

THE MADABA MAP

On the floor of a sixth-century church in Madaba, Jordan, there is a mosaic map of the Holy Land, including Jerusalem as it was in Hadrian's time.

Formed of hundreds of pieces of colored stone, the map is oriented with the eastern direction at the top instead of north, as was the custom of mapmakers at that time. On this map of Aelia Capitolina, it is easy to see the Roman gate as the most important entrance to the city. This is the same gate that has been found under the present-day Damascus Gate. Beyond the gate, the map shows a large paved plaza with a Roman column in the center, which perhaps supported a statue of Hadrian. Archaeologists have never found traces of this column, even though at one point it would have been the first thing that visitors to the city saw. The long Cardo with its rows of columns is clearly visible in the map, as well as other gates and walls. The Church of the Holy Sepulchre, which was built later in the city's Roman era, is also visible with its distinctive rotunda.

A sixth-century mosaic of colored stone found in Saint George's Church at Madaba, Jordan, depicts a map of ancient Jerusalem.

ROMAN TEMPLES

As a conquered Roman city, Aelia Capitolina was also expected to replace the religion of the Jewish people with that of Rome. The Romans wanted to displace Jewish and Christian worship at the two holy sites in the city. To accomplish this, Emperor Hadrian built two temples: one to the goddess Aphrodite on the site of Jesus' crucifixion and the other honoring the god Jupiter on the site of the First and Second Temples on the Temple Mount. Some historical sources also refer to a statue of Hadrian himself that stood on the Temple Mount. This defiling of one of the holiest places of the Jewish religion sparked one of many uprisings that the Romans continually had to subdue during their occupation of Jerusalem.

With the basic structures of Roman domination in place, Aelia Capitolina grew as more Roman soldiers and their families established homes there. The Romans then turned their attention to building areas of their city for entertainment. Aelia Capitolina had theaters, a hippodrome, and baths, which were a central part of Roman life not only for cleanliness but also for entertainment and socializing. Traces of a large bathhouse have been uncovered near a corner of the Temple Mount, probably for the use of the Tenth Legion soldiers. Another

An illustration dramatizes the conversion of Roman emperor Constantine I to Christianity in A.D. 312.

bathhouse was located near the center of Aelia Capitolina but has left no trace. The theater and hippodrome have yet to be found by modern archaeologists, but two stone "tickets" to the theater were found in an excavation on the Temple Mount.

THE END OF AELIA CAPITOLINA

The two centuries in which Jerusalem was known as Aelia Capitolina were the quietest and least known in its history, since the city at that point was a sleepy little colony of importance to no one except the Jewish people, who were banned from it. Many Jewish people did brave a penalty of death to visit the site of their destroyed temple. Christians were allowed to live in the city and the growing interest in the life of a man called Jesus made it a place of pilgrimage for them.

During his rule, the new Roman emperor Constantine, who had been converted to Christianity in A.D. 312, sparked renewed interest in the city of Aelia Capitolina. Christianity became the official religion of the Roman Empire, replacing the traditional worship of gods and goddesses, and Jerusalem once again reverted to its original name. Jews and Christians alike now saw Jerusalem as their Holy City and made pilgrimages there, and the city once again became a focal point for people from all over the Christian world. No longer a sleepy, forgotten Roman provincial town, Jerusalem entered a new era, not only as a Jewish and Christian holy place but also as an emerging holy city for the Muslim faith as well. This would lead to the construction of even more layers of the city of Jerusalem.

MUSLIM
JERUSALEM

3

After years of Roman rule and the increasing importance of the Christian religion in Jerusalem, the city was once again besieged in A.D. 638. The followers of a new religion, originating in Arabia and based on the teachings of the prophet Muhammad, were quietly taking hold over the Arabian Peninsula (present-day Saudia Arabia). After successfully conquering Byzantium and Persia, the Muslim caliph Omar entered Jerusalem in 638. Peaceful negotiations took place between Omar and the Byzantine emperor Heraclius, and the city surrendered into Omar's hands, without bloodshed. Under Muslim rule, Christians in Jerusalem were allowed to continue practicing their religion, and Jews were once again allowed to live in the city.

JERUSALEM AS A HOLY MUSLIM CITY

Jerusalem was holy to the Islamic faith because the Temple Mount was said to be the place where Muhammad was carried to one night from his home in Mecca, and from where he ascended through the seven levels of Heaven into the presence of the Almighty God. When the caliph Omar entered Jerusalem after his siege, he asked to be taken to the Temple Mount, the site of Muhammad's holy journey. The Christian patriarch of Jerusalem, named Sophronius, was reluctant to take Omar there because Christians had been using the site as a waste dump, since it had no religious significance for them at that time. When Omar saw the condition of the area, he was said to have been so shocked that he forced Sophronius to crawl through the mud and debris on his hands and knees, as punishment for the Christians' treatment of a site that was so holy to the Muslims. Other

The prophet Muhammad, the founder of the religion of Islam, mounted at the head of his followers.

stories tell of Omar himself gathering up dirt and rubbish in the hem of his robe and tossing it over the side of the Temple Mount into the valley below, with his men doing the same with their garments, shields, baskets, and pitchers, until the sacred rock reappeared.

This sacred rock was the same rock that King David had acquired in Jerusalem's earliest days, and where his first rough temple once stood, containing the Ark of the Covenant. It had also been a part of Solomon's and Herod's temples. The Islamic faith held it holy based on its role in Muhammad's journey to Heaven, and it is said that as Muhammad ascended, the jealous rock tried to follow him to Paradise and Archangel Gabriel fended it off, pushing it back to Earth and leaving his handprint etched into the stone. This was the main reason why Omar decided to build a mosque on the Temple Mount, although it is also said that building a mosque on a site so holy to two other religions emphasized the victory of Islam over Judaism.

Here Omar first built a rough four-sided, wooden mosque. The mosque was constructed by raising beams and rubble on the remains of some of the First and Second Temple ruins. It could hold three thousand men at once, according to the accounts of traveling pilgrims at that time.

THE DOME OF THE ROCK

In A.D. 687, Omar's successor, a caliph named Abd al-Malik, decided to replace Omar's primitive mosque with a magnificent building that would become the Kubbat al-Sakhra, or Dome of the Rock. Part of this decision was based on the need to bring more religious pilgrims and their gold into Jerusalem, instead of Mecca and Medina, the two sites considered holier to the Muslims than Jerusalem.

Abd al-Malik used the best Byzantine and Persian architects and craftsmen at his disposal. He wanted to create a shrine so magnificent that not only would it be unsurpassed in both the Islamic and the Christian worlds but it would also dazzle and inspire pilgrims.

FIRST STEPS IN CONSTRUCTION

Abd al-Malik, who was living in Damascus at the time, traveled to Jerusalem to inspect the site of his new mosque. The Temple Mount area that once surrounded Herod's wonderful temple—with its remaining masonry walls and broad, flat plaza—was a perfect place to build and would come to be known to Muslims as the Haram al-Sharif, or Noble Sanctuary. Abd al-Malik came here to view the area and speak with the two men who would oversee the project—one known for great scholarship and wisdom and the other a native of Jerusalem. He ordered them to first build a model, or prototype, of the Dome of the Rock based on their designs. If he liked the model, he would then allow them to begin work on the great mosque itself.

This model of the Dome of the Rock still stands near the great mosque. Now called the Dome of the Chain, the model was first used to house the treasure necessary to finance the building of the huge mosque, and later as a storehouse for the spices and perfumes that were used in the Dome of the Rock during worship. It was given its current name because it also

The Dome of the Rock complex covers the rock of Moriah, the site where Muhammad is believed to have ascended to heaven.

once held a length of chain called King David's Chain of Judgment, which could supposedly only be grasped by innocent people and would evade the touch of the guilty.

Abd al-Malik evidently approved of the small model, and ordered construction to begin on the Dome of the Rock in A.D. 687.

It was finished in only four years, and the dome as it stands to-day has changed very little since the day it was completed.

THE DESIGN OF THE DOME OF THE ROCK

The Dome of the Rock's design is based on the Roman design of a dome supported by an eight-sided base. Using the secret

THE PALESTINE EXPLORATION FUND

Many archaeologists working in Jerusalem have had troublesome relationships with the Muslim people who control the Dome of the Rock and the site of the Jewish temples. In the 1860s, the Palestine Exploration Fund (PEF) was founded in England to further research into archaeology and history in biblical Palestine. One of the most important expeditions funded by the PEF was undertaken by Lieutenant Charles Warren of the British Royal Engineers. His instructions were to investigate Jerusalem: the site of the temple, the line of walls enclosing the ancient city, and the authenticity of the traditional site of the Holy Sepulchre.

Warren conducted his work at great personal risk because of the shaky relationships between the Christian British explorers in his party and the Muslims controlling Jerusalem at that time, and their reluctance or even refusal to allow him too near the Dome of the Rock and its environs. At one point, the pounding of the sledgehammers used by Warren's men enraged the worshipers in the mosque above them, and they showered the workers with stones. Warren finally rented privately owned land near the Temple Mount and then tunneled toward it, tracing the walls of Herod's temple more than ninety feet below ground. Over all, he dug twenty-seven separate shafts and traced much of the northern and southern limits of the city over four months. In this way Warren and his men were able to define the topography of ancient Jerusalem, recognize the work of Herod on the temple platform, and explore the city's ancient water systems. He raised public interest in the work of the Palestine Exploration Fund so greatly with his discoveries that the fund received over $95,000 in contributions from the public.

engineering formulas of the ancient architects and engineers who built the Egyptian pyramids and the temples of Greece, the mosque was designed to be a unified geometric whole where each part of the building is related to every other part in a definite proportion. The floor plan of the Dome of the Rock is made up of two sets of interlocking squares, the inner set being the circumference of the dome itself and the outer set the size of the exterior of the octagonal (eight-sided) base.

Professor K.A.C. Cresswell, a British authority on Muslim architecture, wrote about the geometric concept of the Dome of the Rock:

> Under a scheme whereby the size of every part is related to every other part in some definite proportion . . . a building instead of being a collection of odd notes becomes a harmonious chord in stones, a sort of living crystal; and after all it really is not strange that harmonies of this sort should appeal to us through our sight, just as chords in music appeal to us through our hearing. Some of the ratios involved . . . are fundamentals in time and space, they go right down to the very basis of our nature, and of the physical universe in which we live and move.[10]

The design of the Dome of the Rock went far beyond the usual construction techniques of the time, with every aspect of the building thought out in a geometric relationship intended to make worshipers experience the harmony and order of God's universe, and of life itself.

THE INTERIOR DESIGN

The interior of the Dome of the Rock was divided into three rings. The first ring surrounded the rock itself, located directly below the huge dome. The design was intended to make the rock appear to be leaping toward paradise, as it tried to do in the Muslim legend. A latticework screen of ebony wood and a brocade curtain that could be drawn aside encircled the rock. Around this was a circle of piers and columns that supported the rotunda.

Surrounding this center ring were two more rings of piers and columns whose lines paralleled the eight faces of the exterior wall. Four of these exterior sides had entranceways, which

An overhead view of the sacred rock in the Dome of the Rock mosque.

were aligned to the four points of the compass. The interior columns were sculpted from fine marble, which was variegated and veined. These had been scavenged from the ruins of Christian churches leveled by the Persians seventy years before, and so most of them are of different sizes and some even have crosses carved into their surfaces. Magnificent stone arches span all the columns, connecting them and supporting the dome.

The decoration of the mosque's interior was a series of mosaic designs that still glow brightly today. The Byzantine craftsmen of the time were experts at mosaic work, in which millions of colored cubes of stone are arranged to create patterns in bright yellow, red, blue, green, black, gray, and gold. Islamic art does not allow the representation of people or animals, so all designs must consist of plants and vegetation or geometric designs. These mosaics were set so that the golden cubes of the background at the base, or drum, of the dome are tilted forward 30 degrees, making them appear to be brighter than the other motifs. On another section of the octagon, the background cubes are flat while the design cubes are tilted forward, making them stand out. Painted plaster and jewels also adorned the interior of the mosque, as well as elegant calligraphy telling the story of Muhammad's ascension and other Islamic scripture. A great chandelier of five hundred lamps hung above the rock itself. There was even a small shrine beside the rock that was said to hold a hair from Muhammad's beard. The interior itself appears to be larger than the exterior of the Dome of the Rock, and the combined elements of the sanctuary were calculated to inspire awe and reverence.

DECORATING THE EXTERIOR

The exterior of the Dome of the Rock, constructed of white veined marble, was also decorated with multicolored mosaics, just as the inside was, uniting the octagonal base and the dome in sparkling color. The lower drum of the dome was encircled with tiles, including panes of clear green glass that let light into the interior.

The exterior of the dome was originally covered in gold. It is said that the caliph's workmen were so economical that they reported a sum of one hundred thousand gold dinars, the monetary unit in Jerusalem, still unspent at the completion of the Dome of the Rock. Abd al-Malik generously offered it to his overseers as a gift for a job well done, but they refused. Instead, they added an amount of personal gold taken from the ornaments of their wives, and the combined gold was melted down and used to gild the dome. Later travelers would write of the blazing gold of this dome in the sun, which could be seen from long distances away. Two huge coverings of felt and animal skins were used to protect the finish of the dome during the rain, snow, and wind of winter.

Abd al-Malik succeeded in creating a monument to the Islamic religion that was unsurpassed in beauty and attracted pilgrims to Jerusalem for worship. This led to a golden period in Jerusalem when much of the world journeyed there to either the great golden dome or to the sacred Christian sites. As a result, the city thrived on the pilgrims' wealth and piety.

THE DOME IN DISREPAIR

Over the years since its construction, the exterior mosaics of the Dome of the Rock have suffered terribly from the harsh weather.

EXCAVATING UNDER THE DOME OF THE ROCK

According to old but persistent legends, the treasure of King Solomon and perhaps even the Ark of the Covenant are still hidden beneath the Temple Mount. This has led to many attempts to find these treasures, whether for archaeological reasons or personal gain.

In 1908, a Swedish scholar named Valter Juvelius claimed to have decoded a cryptic message in the Bible that revealed the secret hiding place of King Solomon's treasure. Based on this information, a young Englishman, Montague Brownslow Parker, arranged an expedition to Jerusalem in 1909. Parker disguised his treasure hunt as a serious archaeological expedition and began two years of searching for the secret entrance to the cave of Solomon's treasure. He enlisted the help of tunnel engineers who had worked on London's new underground railway and even consulted a psychic to help him locate the passage.

Parker felt sure that the entrance lay in one particular section of the Temple Mount, but since it was within the boundaries of the Dome of the Rock and therefore out of bounds for anyone not of the Muslim faith, Parker found it necessary to bribe two of the highest-ranking officials in the city. He was allowed to commit the ultimate sacrilege of digging in holy ground.

On April 17, 1911, Parker and his men disguised themselves as Arabs and descended a stairway located under the Dome of the Rock to an underground chamber where a slab of stone covered a mysterious depression. Parker and his men began to work at the stone with pickaxes, but the noise alerted a mosque attendant who was not informed of the arrangement made with the two officials. He rushed into the street to raise the alarm at the desecration of the mosque.

As the news spread, it turned into rumors. Some said that the foreigners had found and made off with the Ark of the Covenant, others said they had stolen King Solomon's crown, and still others claimed they had stolen the Sword of Muhammad. Parker and his associates barely managed to slip out of Jerusalem and sail for home from the port city of Jaffa, lucky to escape with their lives, but without the treasure they had hoped to find.

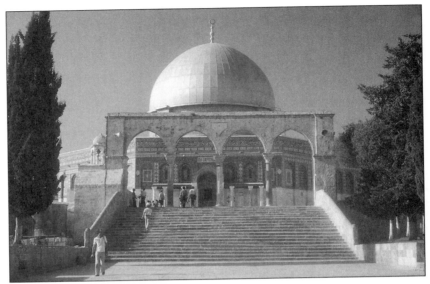

An exterior view of the Dome of the Rock complex shows the workmanship and influence of Byzantine craftsmen.

When the building cycled through a period of use as a Christian church, eager pilgrims chipped away at the rock for souvenirs. Skilled mosaic craftsmen were no longer available to repair the mosque to its original glory.

By the time the sultan Suleiman, known to the West as "the Magnificent" and in the East as "the Lawgiver" came to Jerusalem in 1537, the dome was in dire need of repair. Suleiman began a campaign to restore and beautify the holy site, and the rest of the city. It is said that he financed these repairs with a thousand purses of gold.

Suleiman commanded the tile makers of Kashan, in Persia, to create nearly fifty thousand ceramic tiles to cover the outside of the Dome of the Rock. The tiles were decorated with intricate designs of diamonds, stars, leaves and intertwined stems, lilies, and lotuses, all in brilliant turquoise, blue, black, brown, and green. Restorations of these tiles are still in place today, although when craftsmen were told to reproduce similar tiles in later years, they were unable to meet the same high standards of color and workmanship as the sixteenth-century men of Kashan.

Suleiman also restored the doors of the mosque and added new stained glass windows with floral designs to the interior drum of the dome, which filtered the light from the original green glass blocks into beautiful colors.

In 1917, an English architect named Ernest Richmond did a survey of the Dome of the Rock, which had yet again fallen into terrible disrepair with a huge number of tiles missing from the walls. He found that a minimum of twenty-six thousand new tiles would be needed to rescue the structure. These tiles were installed, financed by the British, who were overseeing Jerusalem at that time, and once again the beautiful exterior was saved from ruin.

A total restoration effort was done between 1958 and 1964, and the gift of a new durable covering of anodized gilt aluminum for the dome's exterior from King Hussein of Jordan, have made the Dome of the Rock just as beautiful today as it was when it was first built.

THE AL-AKSA MOSQUE

The Dome of the Rock was primarily a shrine, constructed to protect the holy rock. While Muslims could worship within the dome, it became necessary to construct an additional mosque to accommodate the numbers of pilgrims and other faithful Muslims who came to Jerusalem to visit the dome. To handle the vast crowds of worshipers who wished to pray there daily, the Al-Aksa Mosque was constructed, and is still the primary place of worship for devout Muslims in Jerusalem.

The caliph Waleed, Abd al-Malik's son, built the silver-domed Al-Aksa Mosque in the early eighth century, at the southwestern end of the temple compound. Only a few of the stone pillars in the colonnade east of the Al-Aksa dome are original to the first building, which was destroyed by earthquakes twice in its first sixty years. In 1034, the caliph Al-Zahir reconstructed the Al-Aksa Mosque. He was responsible for rebuilding the dome and the seven northern doors of the rectangular house of worship, where five thousand people may worship at one time. It is said that the original gold and silver covering of the doors were stripped to finance the repair of the mosque after an earthquake, and that more columns from ruined churches in the vicinity were used in the rebuilding.

Saladin, a later Muslim ruler, restored the Al-Aksa again after it was used by the crusaders as a church and headquarters. He decorated the dome with mosaics and added a beautiful *mihrab*, which is a niche reserved for the imam who leads the prayer during worship in the mosque. He also marbled the floors, decorated the upper interior walls with mosaics, and added an intricately carved pulpit in 1187.

This same pulpit was destroyed by fire in 1969, when a fanatical tourist, Dennis Rohan, set fire to the mosque because of what he believed was a call from God to return the temple area to the Jews, as described in this account:

> Rohan . . . entered the Haram and walked to the mosque, where the guard let Rohan go in by himself. Rohan strode to the inlaid cedar pulpit, brought by Saladin eight hundred years before to celebrate driving the Crusaders from the Holy Land. From his knapsack, he took a couple of containers of kerosene, soaked a scarf, laid it across one of the pulpit's wooden stairs, and lit it. Leaving the mosque [he] began running when he heard a scream of pure agony behind him. Inside the building, flames spread to the carpets and rafters. Sixteen fire trucks battled the blaze for hours. The firefighters also had to struggle with an angry mob of Muslims, some of whom were convinced the Jews were spraying gasoline to feed the flames.[11]

CITY WALLS AND GATES

Besides the beautiful structures of the Dome of the Rock and the Al-Aksa Mosque, the other great contribution made to Jerusalem during the Muslim era were the walls and gates that encircle the city, which can still be seen and walked on today. Suleiman the Magnificent was responsible for this addition during the years A.D. 1536 to 1542.

The city wall today is a two-and-a-half-mile perimeter, built in most cases over the remains of earlier walls. It contains six of Suleiman's original gates as well as several other nonfunctional gates that have been bricked up and sealed. The walls enclose the four quarters of Jerusalem's Old City—the Jewish, Armenian, Muslim, and Christian quarters—as well as the Temple Mount and the Dome of the Rock.

THE KNIGHTS TEMPLAR

During the Crusades, when Christian knights from Europe took control of Jerusalem from the Muslims, the Dome of the Rock was renamed the Templum Domini, reconsecrated to Christianity and crowned with a huge golden cross. Pilgrims to the city were even told that the Templum Domini was the temple that Solomon had built, and the place where Jesus had preached.

European knights attack Muslim fortifications during the Crusades.

In changing the Dome of the Rock to a Christian church, many of the Arabic inscriptions inside the building were plastered over and replaced with jeweled paintings of Jesus and mosaics depicting scenes from the Scriptures. Masons actually carved steps into the sacred rock itself and built an altar above it, and chips from the rock were sold as coveted relics, a practice that only stopped when the rock was paved over with marble for protection, sometime between 1099–1187 A.D.

The Al-Aksa Mosque became the headquarters and barracks of the new aristocratic order of the Knights Templar, who stored arms and provisions nearby and stabled their horses in the huge underground cavern beneath the mosque that they dubbed Solomon's Stables. The Templars became one of the wealthiest and most powerful organizations of its time.

The Templum Domini, the mother church of the knights and the symbol of their order, influenced the design of many churches that were built at that time in Europe and England, with the same octagonal shape crowned by a dome. The most famous example is the Christian Temple Church in London.

All of the city's gates were designed in the same style, with a straight or slightly curved lintel (the section just above the door opening), with an Arabic inscription set inside a higher broken arch. Originally all the gates had an L-shaped entry that worked well when all goods were carried into the city on pack animals, but needed to be modified once wheeled traffic developed. Suleiman gave all six gates official names, but these vary according to the language and the religious community using them.

The Jaffa Gate was named for the road that leads northwest from Jerusalem to the city of Jaffa, which is now a part of the modern city of Tel Aviv, on the coast of the Mediterranean Sea. Built in 1538, it still has the original L-shaped opening for pedestrians and a larger entrance for vehicles, which was straightened in 1898 to accommodate the coach of the visiting German kaiser Wilhelm. The Jaffa Gate is also on the border of Israel and Jordan, and has been closed many times during political uprisings. Beside the gate are the graves of two Turkish architects who were hanged by Suleiman when they failed to

Cars pass through the Jaffa Gate, named for the coastal city northwest of Jerusalem to which the road leads.

include Mount Zion, the site of King David's grave and the Last Supper of Jesus, within the city walls. Suleiman wanted to ensure equal protection for all religions, and when he realized that these Christian holy sites had been excluded, he had the architects executed. However, another story says that Suleiman was so pleased with the work the architects did that he had them killed so they would never be able to build anything greater for anyone else.

The southern Zion Gate, built in 1540, was heavily damaged in the fighting of the 1967 war that reunified Jerusalem. Nearby, also on the southern section of the wall, is the Dung Gate, named for a dump that was once located here just outside the walls. It was a very narrow gate, just a service access, but was widened after World War II.

On the eastern wall is St. Stephen's Gate, also called the Lion's Gate because of the lion decorations carved in the stone. Legends say that Suleiman dreamed he would be eaten by lions if he did not rebuild the walls of Jerusalem. This gate also had an L-shaped entry that was modified by the British during their occupation of Jerusalem in the 1940s, in order to provide better vehicle access to an Austrian hospital located there.

On the northern wall is Herod's Gate, where it is believed Jesus passed through on his way to see King Herod. When the crusaders conquered Jerusalem in 1099, Herod's Gate was their first point of control in the city. Also on the northern wall is the Damascus Gate, the largest gate in Jerusalem. It is under this gate that archaeologists uncovered the remains of a Roman gate from the Aelia Capitolina era.

The Golden Gate, located on the eastern wall, overlooks a Muslim cemetery. Suleiman bricked up the Golden Gate because it was said that the Messiah would one day pass through this gate and liberate the city from his people, the Ottomans, and return it to the Christians.

The newest gate of present-day Jerusalem is called the New Gate, built in 1887 to provide better access to the Christian quarter of the city.

THE LEGACY OF SULEIMAN

Because of his efforts to improve and restore the city, Suleiman is responsible for much of what can still be seen of the city's history in modern Jerusalem. The crusaders also contributed to the landscape of buildings that are Jerusalem's trademark, and to understand their contribution, it is necessary to go back in time before Suleiman and to explore Christian Jerusalem after the Romans.

4

CHRISTIAN JERUSALEM

Before Islam and its possession of Jerusalem, there was a period of time when the city was still a Roman colony, but one that practiced Christianity. In A.D. 324 Aelia Capitolina, as Jerusalem was then called, came under the rule of Emperor Constantine, the first Roman emperor to convert to Christianity. The old gods and goddesses of the Romans were abandoned, and Christianity became the official state religion.

THE ROMAN CHRISTIANS

Constantine became passionately involved with Christianity and called a council of all the various sects and churches in A.D. 325 to settle disputes from all parts of the empire. Constantine's mother, Empress Helena, was also a convert to Christianity, and accompanied him to this council. There she met one of the delegates, Bishop Macarius of Aelia Capitolina. He spoke with her about the sad condition of many of the holy sites in Aelia Capitolina that were linked with Jesus. She was so saddened by his report that she resolved to visit the city. She was in her seventies, which was an advanced age for anyone at that time, let alone someone about to undertake an arduous journey. Empress Helena embarked on this pilgrimage in A.D. 326 with the blessings, authority, and money of her son, the emperor.

Empress Helena, together with Bishop Macarius, identified the locations of many of the most holy sites of Jesus' last days. The sites they chose are the traditional Christian sites still revered today. Empress Helena even claimed to have discovered the actual cross on which Jesus was crucified, complete with the nails that pierced Jesus' hands and feet, and the traditional inscription,

In A.D. 326 Empress Helena, the mother of Constantine, set out to identify and mark the holiest Christian sites of ancient Jerusalem.

sarcastically written by the Romans, proclaiming Jesus to be "King of the Jews." It was after the empress's trip that the name of the city reverted back to Jerusalem, because the city was once again being revered for its associations with Jesus, and that was the city's name in Jesus' time.

NEW SHRINES

Following the identification of the sacred Christian sites by his mother, Constantine decided to erect appropriate shrines to mark them. On the site of Golgotha, the hill where Jesus was said to have been crucified, and the location of his rock tomb, the Roman emperor Hadrian had built a pagan temple to Venus, partly to show the Roman domination over the Christians of the time. Constantine had the temple razed, although the original church he constructed still had some of the columns of the Roman Cardo street in front of its steps. Enclosing the hill and the tomb, he constructed a magnificent church, the first Church of the Holy Sepulchre.

Emperor Constantine's church was actually a collection of buildings located within a rectangular area. The most outstanding feature, which still exists today, was the Rotunda of the Anastasis, a circular church with the Sepulchre (tomb of Jesus) in the center, surrounded by columns and topped by a huge dome. Adjoining this building to the east was a cloistered open court, and in its center was the traditional rock of Golgotha, where Jesus was crucified. Nearby was another church, the Martyrium, where services were held. Beneath this church was a disused cistern, which later became, and is still called, the Crypt of the Finding of the Cross, commemorating Empress Helena's discovery of the cross of Jesus.

Constantine's church became one of the most venerated sites in the Christian world, and one of the most powerful attractions for Christian pilgrims. Where once Jerusalem had been a place of pilgrimage for devout Jews to visit the location of their temples, by A.D. 400 it was also a destination for Christian pilgrims to worship at the sites of Jesus' last days.

The Church of the Holy Sepulchre, as built by Constantine, was destroyed by the Persians in A.D. 614 and restored on a smaller scale a few years later. In the year 1010 it was destroyed again, but was rebuilt in 1048. It was not until the crusaders came to Jerusalem that the entire shrine was rebuilt under a single roof in 1144.

Constantine was also responsible for constructing the Church of Eleona on the Mount of Olives, on the site where Jesus was said to have revealed God's mysteries to his disciples. The remains of this church were discovered in 1910 during archaeological excavations and are today covered by the Basilica of the Sacred Heart. Constantine and those who followed him were also responsible for constructing monasteries, convents, and hospices to accommodate the growing number of monks, nuns, and pilgrims in the city. Until the Muslims besieged the city in A.D. 638, Jerusalem was almost entirely Christian and Jews were still barred from the city except for one day a year, the anniversary of the destruction of the Second Temple, when Jews were permitted to visit the temple site and mourn over its ruins.

THE CRUSADES

Christians and Muslims managed to occupy Jerusalem together in the years of Muslim rule, from A.D. 638 until 1099, but as the Islamic population grew in the East, it began to spread and overtake the Byzantine Christian territories. This shattered the peaceful coexistence of the Muslims and Christians in Jerusalem. In 1009, an Egyptian caliph named al-Hakim destroyed the Church of the Holy Sepulchre and began to persecute Christians and Jews. Christians who attempted to make the important pilgrimage to Jerusalem and its holy sites were prevented from

A TRAVELER VISITS THE HOLY SEPULCHRE

In 1836 John Lloyd Stephens, a U.S. lawyer and archaeologist, visited the Holy Land and the city of Jerusalem. He chronicled his experiences in a book, *Incidents of Travel in Egypt, Arabia Petraea, and the Holy Land.* In it he describes his experiences while visiting the Church of the Holy Sepulchre, illustrating the condition of the church at that time and the difficulty of experiencing a spiritual connection with a holy place amid the crowds of tourists and pilgrims:

> The holy sepulchre, as in the days when all the chivalry of Europe armed to wrest it from them, is still in the hands of the infidels; and it would have made the sword of an old crusader leap from its scabbard to behold a haughty Turk, with the air of a lord and master, standing sentinel at the door and with his long mace beating and driving back the crowd of struggling Christians. As soon as the door opened, a rush was made for [the] entrance; and as I was in the front rank, before the impetus ceased, amid a perfect storm of pushing, yelling and shouting, I was carried almost headlong into the body of the church. The press continued behind, hurrying me along and kicking off my shoes; and in a state of desperate excitement both of mind and body, utterly unsuited to the place and time, I found myself standing over the so-called tomb of Christ, where, to enhance the incongruity of the scene, at the head of the sepulchre stood a long-bearded monk with a plate in his hand, receiving paras [a Turkish copper coin] from the pilgrims. My dress marked me as a different person from the miserable, beggarly crowd before me; and expecting a better contribution from me, at the tomb of him who had pronounced that all men are equal in the sight of God, with an expression of contempt . . . and with kicks, cuffs, and blows, he drove back those before me and gave me a place at the head of the sepulchre. My feelings were painfully disturbed, as well by the manner of my entrance as by the irreverent demeanor of the monk; and disappointed, disgusted, and sick at heart, while hundreds were still struggling for admission, I turned away and left the church. A warmer imagination than mine could perhaps have seen, in a white marble sarcophagus, "the sepulchre hewn out of a rock," and in the fierce struggling of these barefoot pilgrims the devotion of sincere and earnest piety, burning to do homage in the holiest of places; but I could not.

entering the city or even killed. At the end of the eleventh century, a message supposedly written by the pope was sent out as a call to arms:

> Let all Christians know that news has come from the east to the seat of the apostles that the church of the Holy Sepulchre has been destroyed from roof to foundations at the impious hands of the pagans. This destruction has plunged the entire church and the city of Rome into deep grief and distress.
>
> The whole world is in mourning, and the people tremble, breathing deep sighs. Never should our eyes be blessed with sleep, or our hearts with joy, if we ever read in the prophets, in the Psalms or in the fathers that the Redeemer's tomb would be destroyed.
>
> Therefore, let this Christian intention be known: that we, personally, if it pleases the Lord, desire to setout from these shores with any Romans, Italians, or Tuscans who wish to come with us. With the Lord's help we intend to kill all these enemies and to restore the Redeemer's Holy Sepulchre. Nor, my sons, are you to fear the sea's turbulence, nor dread the fury of war, for God has promised that whoever loses the present life for the sake of Christ will gain another life which he will never lose. For this is not a battle for an earthly kingdom, but for the eternal Lord.[12]

These words launched the First Crusade, one of the bloodiest episodes in Jerusalem's long history. Knights, professional soldiers, and common people alike took an oath vowing to fight on until Jerusalem and other holy places were once again in Christian hands, and in return they were promised forgiveness of their sins and a place in Heaven. People who joined the Crusades were said to have "taken the cross" and wore its symbol proudly on their tunics. The People's Crusade, made up of common men and women, left for the Holy Land under the leadership of Peter the Hermit, a preacher who so inspired his followers that some were convinced he was a saint. In the end, three armies set out from Europe toward Constantinople and Jerusalem. It took nearly two years for the crusaders to reach the Holy Land.

Peter the Hermit exhorts a crowd to take up the cause of reclaiming Jerusalem from Muslim control. Peter is credited as the leader of the First Crusade.

They finally reached the city of Jerusalem in June of 1099. The crusaders began attacking right away, but they made little progress until they were able to construct siege machinery. There was still a shortage of trees in the area, and some of the ships that had transported the crusaders from Europe were broken up and hauled to Jerusalem for their wood. A crusader named Radulph of Caen wrote of the near miracle where his lord, Tancred, discovered a load of timber in a cave:

> Tancred was suffering from severe dysentery, but did not spare himself from riding out [in search of wood] even though he could barely stay on his horse. This nuisance kept forcing him to dismount, go away from the group and find a hiding-place. . . . He therefore sought concealment . . . in a deep recess beneath a hollow rock, surrounded by trees and bristling shade. Good gracious! Who but God? . . . He it was who healed the army

through the illness of one knight, who brought strength out of weakness, and from a vile affliction made a remedy more precious than gold. For while Tancred was relieving himself there, he faced a cave in the rock opposite, where four hundred timbers lay open to view.[13]

The crusaders built siege towers, battering rams, and mangonels (stone throwers) for their assault on the city walls. Before the actual battle, they paraded barefoot around the city walls, carrying holy relics and praying to God for courage. The Turks watching them from the city walls looked on in amazement and shouted insults. But on July 15, 1099, the crusaders breached the walls of Jerusalem and hoisted their flags over the city, including the Dome of the Rock and the Al-Aksa Mosque.

A BLOODY RAMPAGE

Unfortunately, the crusaders' entry into Jerusalem was not peaceful. As one eyewitness wrote:

> On Friday 15 July 1099, early in the morning we attacked the city from all sides. . . . One of our knights climbed up on to the wall of the city. As soon as he had climbed it, all the defenders of the city fled along the walls and through the city, and our men . . . chased after them, killing them and dismembering them as far as the Temple of Solomon. And in that place there was such slaughter that we were up to our ankles in their blood.
>
> In the morning our men climbed cautiously on to the roof of the Temple and attacked the Saracens [Muslims], both male and female, and beheaded them with unsheathed swords. The other Saracens threw themselves from the Temple.[14]

This bloodshed ushered in eighty-seven years of rule by crusaders in Jerusalem, when it became known as the Crusader Kingdom of Jerusalem, ruled by knights who were chosen to become kings there. Once again Jerusalem was an important international capital.

BUILDING A CHRISTIAN JERUSALEM

Under the crusaders' Christian rule, Jerusalem underwent a spree of construction, although the actual shape of the city within the walls stayed much the same as it was during Roman rule. Churches, convents, monasteries, hospices, and housing for the clergy sprang up all over the city. Most of these buildings were concentrated in the quadrant of the city that is still referred to as the Christian quarter. One of the greatest Christian landmarks in the city was located here, the Via Dolorosa ("Walk of Sorrow"). The walk had its beginnings in the renaming of the Ecco Homo Arch, which was called the Gate Dolorous in cru-

The crusaders' bloody conquest of Jerusalem ushered in eighty-seven years of Christian rule.

THE CHILDREN'S CRUSADE

One of the saddest episodes of the Crusades is that of the Children's Crusade in A.D. 1212. In the summer of that year, groups of children were chosen to liberate the Holy Land from the infidels. Children were thought to personify the first martyrs of the Christian faith because of the innocent children who were murdered by the Roman king Herod, who tried to prevent the birth of a Jewish king by killing every newborn child in Jerusalem at the time of Jesus' birth. The children were also to represent a sacrifice from a penitent society, and in their innocence they would be able to capture Jerusalem unarmed.

The thousands of children, aged ten to eighteen, were joined by other crusaders, mostly from lower-order clergymen but also including some married women and unmarried girls. They sailed to the Holy Land with no money and few provisions. Some of the ships they sailed on were wrecked and the children drowned at sea. Others reached Rome, only to be told that the church would not authorize their crusade, and they disbanded. Few managed to make their way back home. Most were abused or abducted and sold as slaves, and others roamed the country alone and hungry. Pope Gregory IX had a church constructed on an island near Sardinia, calling it the New Innocents. It contained many graves of children washed up on the island after one of the shipwrecks, and the bodies of some of them were said to have been displayed "incorrupt" to pilgrims, preserved by God exactly as they were when alive.

sader times and had been mistakenly identified as the arch that Jesus stood beneath when he came to be judged by Herod. This walk along the streets and churches of Jerusalem was said to trace the path Jesus took through the city, as he carried his cross to the place where he was crucified. This is still one of Jerusalem's greatest attractions for Christian pilgrims, as they follow the fourteen Stations of the Cross, which are small shrines marking the different places where Jesus stopped or faltered or fell on his journey to his death. The walk ends within the Church of the Holy Sepulchre.

Outside of Jerusalem, in an area now called the New City, there is a fortified monastery built by the crusaders in a vineyard called the Monastery of the Cross. The crusaders built it here because, according to legend, it marks the place where the tree grew from which Jesus' cross was made.

The most important building associated with the crusader era in Jerusalem is the Church of the Holy Sepulchre. The destruction of this Christian holy place was what initially sparked the Crusades, and when the crusaders finally entered Jerusalem, massacred most of the inhabitants, and marched through its empty streets, this church was the first place they went to pray and thank God for their victory.

THE CHURCH OF THE HOLY SEPULCHRE

The crusaders found the Church of the Holy Sepulchre in ruins when they conquered Jerusalem in 1099. When the Egyptian al-Hakim destroyed the church in 1009, it was in the form that Constantine had constructed: a rotunda over the tomb of Jesus, called the Anastasis, and a basilica, with the Rock of Golgotha in an open courtyard. When Empress Helena located Jesus' tomb, it was one of many, cut into a rock hillside much like a cave. Helena had it hewn from the hillside until it stood alone, and then covered it with a small building called the Edicule. Hakim commanded his men to use picks and hammers to destroy the rock tomb, stopping only when it was so covered with debris that it could no longer be seen.

The crusaders united all the separate parts of Constantine's church under one roof, connecting the Rotunda of Anastasis with a classic crusader-era church, characterized by a floor plan with two main aisles intercepting each other like a cross. This also enclosed the Rock of Golgotha and Constantine's entire courtyard within the church. The damaged tomb was covered with marble and then enclosed in the new Edicule. The original rotunda was open to the sky in the center of its dome, and it was necessary to protect the Edicule from wet weather by hanging carpets or draperies above it. The last construction added by the crusaders was a bell tower. The entrance to the church is through a crusader-style doorway, one of two, but the second doorway has been blocked up since it gave access to the tombs of two crusader kings and later rulers in Jerusalem wanted to hide these symbols of the Crusader Kingdom.

The Edicule, believed to house Jesus' tomb, stands in the rotunda of the Church of the Holy Sepulchre.

The crusaders also excavated the crypt of St. Helena, where the cross of Jesus was said to have been found. It is still possible today to see crosses carved into the stone walls of the crypt by pilgrims who visited there during Jerusalem's time as the Crusader Kingdom.

The church suffered further damage and desecration after the crusader era ended, as well as being subjected to inept repairs. In 1808, there was a fire in the church, supposedly started by a monk who then tried to douse it with brandy and only made the fire worse. The rotunda collapsed onto the Edicule, destroying a decorative cupola on top of the tomb and most of the marble and limestone covering. The door into the tomb was blackened and charred, but it managed to protect the interior. After the fire, the Edicule was totally rebuilt in the form it has today.

In 1927, the Church of the Holy Sepulchre was badly shaken by an earthquake, and because of the difficulties in getting all

HOLY RELICS

When Constantine's mother, the empress Helena, journeyed to Jerusalem to find the sites from the life of Jesus, she also found fragments of the true cross that Jesus was crucified on, as well as four of the nails that would have nailed him to the cross. Relics like these were extremely important to faithful Christians, and Helena brought them back to her palace in Rome. However, instead of displaying them in a chapel or church, she found some rather odd uses for the nails. One was made into a diadem, a type of crown, and the other was made into part of a horse's bridle. Helena sent both of these objects to her son, and he used the bridle for his favorite horse.

A fragment of the wood of the Holy Cross was displayed in Jerusalem once a year, for pilgrims to see and touch. In their book *The Quest for the True Cross*, authors Carsten Peter Thiede and Matthew d'Ancona quote Egeria, a fourth-century pilgrim to the Holy Land, as she describes the ceremony that took place when the cross was displayed:

> And so the whole [group of] people goes past the table, everyone bows and touches the wood and the inscription first with the forehead, then with the eyes, and kissing the Cross, they move on. But no one touches it with their hands. On one occasion, however—I do not know when— one of them bit off a piece of the Holy Wood and took it away by theft. And for this reason the deacons stand round and keep watch so that no one dares to do the same again.

After the Crusades, there were many supposed relics brought back to Europe by the crusading knights. Thorns from the crown Jesus wore during his crucifixion were given to many

the different sects to agree to the repairs, the damage was not fully repaired until 1988. An ecumenical council for all the Christian communities decided on a major repair program in 1959. Only the areas that were structurally unsafe were to be replaced. Modern masons were even trained to trim new stones in the old style to match the ancient stones of the church. An illustration of the complicated organization of these repairs is in the restoration of three of the huge pillars supporting the rotunda: The Greek Orthodox sect restored a square pillar that they

King Louis IX of France receives from crusaders the crown of thorns and other holy relics.

churches, as well as items such as a piece of the skeletal finger of one of Jesus' apostles and a section of the wood from the cross of a thief who was crucified at the same time as Jesus. Others claimed to have been given things like the robe that Jesus wore when the Roman soldiers mocked him, and the sponge that was dipped in vinegar to moisten his lips as he was dying. Most of these items were not authentic, but they provided a tangible symbol of faith from the Holy Land for the Christians of the world.

owned, while two other Corinthian pillars were restored by the Armenians.

The Edicule was so badly shaken that it was encased in steel and timber straps, looking much like a cage constructed around the small building. It is possible to see parts of the Edicule walls bulging out between the strapping. Inside, there is the tomb chamber and the Chapel of the Angel. The burial couch where Jesus is said to have lain is covered with marble, and because of the division of the church, there are dividing lines even within these tiny rooms because different sects tend to different areas. At some point the Edicule will need to be rebuilt from the ground up, which will reveal many interesting layers of its history. Archaeologist Martin Biddle has conducted an eleven-year study of the tomb, including both an extensive study of descriptions of the tomb throughout history and modern techniques of computerized photographic imaging, through which he hopes to discover more about the tomb's history and authenticity.

THE CHURCH TODAY

The Church of the Holy Sepulchre perhaps best illustrates the history and the layers of Jerusalem itself over the ages. It is a confusing but memorable hodgepodge of styles and eras, with reused Roman stones and modern stones and crusader construction side by side, as well as blocked-up doorways, tiny chapels to different sects, and parts of Constantine's original church courtyard and gates that can still be found tucked away within ordinary buildings and shops nearby.

The Church of the Holy Sepulchre seems to personify Jerusalem itself, since it has long been the subject of arguments among the major Christian religious sects who feel they have

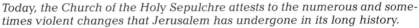

Today, the Church of the Holy Sepulchre attests to the numerous and sometimes violent changes that Jerusalem has undergone in its long history.

claim to the holy ground. The church is shared by six different Christian communities: the Latins, or Roman Catholics; Greek Orthodox; Armenian Orthodox; Syrian Orthodox; Ethiopians; and Copts. Their respective rights to the church are based on an imperial Ottoman decree issued in 1757, which regulates who can do what and where in the church. The Ethiopians' area of control has even been limited to the roof of one of the chapels. This makes renovations and repairs to the church a complicated process, since many different groups must cooperate and work together. Because no group will trust any other with the key to the church, it is opened and closed daily by a local Muslim family who have been its custodians since the seventeenth century.

Visitors to the church today will find themselves in the midst of several different services, with the religious chants and songs of different groups clashing with each other. This echoes the larger picture of the city of Jerusalem itself, a combination of Jews, Christians, and Muslims each attending to their daily life in their own ways, sometimes coexisting peacefully but more often not. This conflict has had an adverse effect on the city, since the political strife of the twenty-first century touches on both Jerusalem's modern constructions and her ancient landmarks.

MODERN
JERUSALEM

Jerusalem today is a city of layers, a city made up of buildings and landscapes as old as King David's city and as recent as the new apartment buildings and neighborhoods being built every day. Crusader buildings were built on the remains of Ottoman and Muslim buildings, on top of Roman structures, on top of the original walls and water tunnels of Solomon and David. Each quarter of the city had its own particular architecture as well, and many of them were crowded with far too many people in far too small a space, with no room for expansion because of the Old City walls. Adding to the overcrowding and the age and poor condition of many of the structures was the constant political strife in the area, a strife that still continues.

JERUSALEM DIVIDED AND UNITED

In 1947, the United Nations decided to divide Palestine into two states, the Jewish state of Israel and the Arab state of Palestine. In 1948 Israel declared itself a nation and Arab Palestinians launched a war against Israel, hoping to reclaim Israel for Palestine. Israel won the war and enlarged its area, forcing many Arabs to leave Jerusalem and move to nearby Arab countries. Jerusalem itself was divided into two sections. The Palestinians lived on the eastern side where most of the holy sites were located, including the Wailing Wall near the site of Herod's temple. The Jewish people lived on the western side, and a barbed wire fence ran through gutted houses and deserted streets to divide the two halves of the city.

In 1966 and 1967, Egypt and other nearby nations attacked Israel, and in 1967 Israel responded by attacking Syria, Jordan,

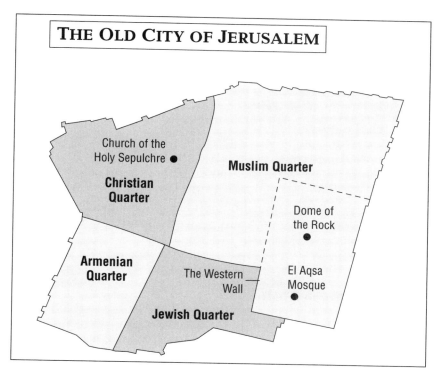

THE OLD CITY OF JERUSALEM

Church of the
Holy Sepulchre ●

Muslim Quarter

Christian
Quarter

Dome of
the Rock
●

Armenian
Quarter

The Western
Wall

El Aqsa
Mosque
●

Jewish Quarter

Iraq, and Egypt. This war only lasted six days, and is still referred to as the Six-Day War. In this war, Israel captured territory
near its borders and reclaimed all of the city of Jerusalem for Israel. The fence dividing the city was torn down, but the informal
division of Jews and Arabs and their living and working neighborhoods remains. Each religion maintains its claims to what it
considers to be its holiest sites in Jerusalem, leading to frequent
conflicts and violence. Holy sites often become targets for destruction, as the city cycles through periods of occupation by different religions.

JERUSALEM'S NEW CITY

After the Six-Day War, there was a building boom of residential
structures outside of the Old City. The idea was to surround
Jerusalem with a ring of suburban residential areas, which
would help to cement the Jewish claim to Jerusalem and protect
the city from Palestinian inhabitants seeking to reclaim it.

Much of modern Jerusalem's development was the result of
a master plan developed in 1968, with the intention of creating

a unified city with a single commercial center. Critics of the plan argued that it would destroy the individuality of the city. Arthur Kutcher, an architect who worked as a planning officer for the city, was critical of the plan, as quoted in the book *Divided Jerusalem: The Struggle for the Holy City*, " 'This unity' [Kutcher] feared, 'was to be imposed . . . at the expense of many aesthetic and environmental qualities.' [Kutcher] and others drew attention to the wrecking of Jerusalem's delicate skylines by many of the new buildings constructed after 1967."[15]

The result is a typical skyline of high-rise hotels and apartment buildings on the outskirts of the ancient city, some out of proportion to their surroundings and even constructed without building permits, as well as some well-planned communities

MOSHE DAYAN'S COLLECTION

Moshe Dayan, one of modern Israel's most famous generals, created one of the biggest private collections of Jerusalem and Holy Land artifacts. In 1954 he made a chance discovery of three-thousand-year-old jars protruding from a stream bank. This launched a passion for ancient relics of his country's past and archaeology, and this passion stayed with him until his death in 1981.

Dayan would either do his own digging for relics in archaeological sites, or purchase them from others, until he had a collection of more than one thousand items that represented a thousand years of history. He displayed many of them in the garden of his home, cleaning and restoring them himself.

Dayan was criticized for his hobby by professionals who claimed that he excavated without a license and failed to properly document his findings. Adding to the controversy was the tendency of local farmers and workers to contact Dayan when they made a discovery, rather than the archaeological authorities. Dayan claimed that much of what he had found would have gone unnoticed or been destroyed by developers if he had not rescued it. Today Moshe Dayan's collection is housed in the Israel Museum in Jerusalem.

with beautiful homes and tree-lined streets. It is said that housing projects in Jerusalem are laboratory experiments, with city planners trying everything from "box" architecture to semi-Oriental homes with numerous arches, in an attempt to create a unique architecture for the city that would match its unique nature.

All of the modern construction in Jerusalem has only added to the city's bewildering mosaic of old and new buildings, of significance to different religions and political groups. Many of these modern sites are often the source of violence, or have been affected by the strife that still engulfs the city.

THE HURVA SYNAGOGUE

One of these sites is the Hurva Synagogue. In 1700, a group of Jews from Poland erected this synagogue in the Jewish Quarter of Jerusalem. They enclosed their synagogue within a compound of roughly forty houses, a study hall, a ritual bath, and a poorhouse. However, the ruling powers in Jerusalem imposed heavy taxes on this group that they could not pay, and so the synagogue was looted and set on fire. Only the shell of the building remained, since it was built of stone, and its name, the Hurva Synagogue, comes from the Hebrew word for ruin, *hurva*.

The synagogue complex was rebuilt in 1864 and the dome became visible above the rooftops of the city. However, in 1948 the Jordanian Arab troops destroyed it yet again during the fighting between Arab and Jewish armies. All that remains of the synagogue today is a single reconstructed arch that was once part of the building's façade, and visitors can wander inside the ruins. Since 1967, when the Israelis recaptured the Old City of Jerusalem, there have been many plans for rebuilding the synagogue, but nothing has been done yet. Hurva Square is one of the few open spaces within the Jewish Quarter and is used as a social center.

THE RUSSIAN COMPOUND

Another area that has been a victim of disagreements between cultures is the Russian compound. One of the first groups of people to settle outside the safety of the walls of Jerusalem was the Russians. Nearly two hundred thousand Russian pilgrims visited Jerusalem every year in the 1800s, and in 1860 the Russians acquired a few acres of land a short distance outside the

The freestanding Arch of Hurva marks the location of the façade of the Hurva Synagogue, erected on this site in 1700.

walls. There they built a nearly self-contained compound to lodge and care for all the Russian pilgrims. In 1864 they built the Cathedral of the Holy Trinity, an unmistakably Russian-style building topped with eight green onion-shaped domes. The bells in this cathedral were brought to Jerusalem in 1856 and were the first to ring out over the city since the crusader period, since before that time the government did not permit the sound of church bells. They also built a consulate, a hospital, and several hospices, or houses, for pilgrims, all enclosed by a wall. It is here that the half-carved column once intended for Herod's Temple was found still attached to the bedrock, and is still visible today.

Today the Russians own only the cathedral. When the British captured Jerusalem in World War I, they declared all of Russia's properties to be enemy institutions and confiscated them. The Soviet Union regained ownership of the compound, but eventually sold off all the other buildings in exchange for shipments of oranges from Israel. The buildings now have other uses, including the Israel Agricultural Ministry and a museum dedicated to the Jewish resistance fighters during the British Mandate period from 1917 to 1948.

YEMIN MOSHE

At the same time that the Russians were building outside the city walls, a rich Jewish philanthropist named Sir Moses Montefiore was so shocked by the crowded and squalid living conditions within the Jewish Quarter that he decided to improve the living standards of the Jews by building a new community also outside the walls. His first project was called Mishkenot Shaananin (meaning "Dwellings of Tranquility") and consisted of a block of sixteen apartments. At first people were reluctant to move outside of the crowded safety of the Old City, fearing that they would be vulnerable to robbery and violence, but by the end of the nineteenth century there was a small community established there, called Yemin Moshe, *Moshe* being the Hebrew word for "Moses," which was Montefiore's first name.

Yemin Moshe was the core from which modern Jerusalem has spread. Characterized by beautiful town houses and cottages built of Jerusalem stone with red roofs, Yemin Moshe is now one of the most expensive places to live in the city. The original Mishkenot Shaananin lodging once had to be offered rent-free to attract tenants, but now it is used as a government guesthouse where famous artists and writers such as Marc Chagall and Saul Bellow have stayed. The Jerusalem branch of the YMCA (Young Men's Christian Association) was built here, designed by the same man who designed the Empire State Building in New York City. It is now one of the most beautiful and elegant buildings in the city. It is richly decorated inside and has a bell tower that provides excellent views of Jerusalem.

Montefiore also wished to provide the Jewish occupants with a means for supporting themselves and being self-sufficient. He constructed a huge windmill so that the inhabitants could grind their own flour and charge Jerusalem residents for the same service, but unfortunately there was rarely enough wind to turn the huge sails. The windmill was used during twentieth-century wars as an Israeli observation post, and its rounded top was destroyed twice by Arab shells and later restored. Yemin Moshe also includes many grassy parks, many of them with public sculptures, ornaments, and fountains.

DESECRATING HOLY SITES

During the Jordanian rule of the Palestinian side of Jerusalem from 1949 until 1967, many important Jewish sites were either off-limits to Jews or were desecrated or destroyed by the Jorda-

A group of Israeli soldiers guards the Western Wall, access to which is disputed by Muslims and Jews.

THE ISRAEL MUSEUM

Also built outside Jerusalem's city walls are many of its museums and government buildings.

Built in 1965 on a ridge overlooking West Jerusalem, the Israel Museum contains some of the most important exhibits of art and archaeology in Israel. It displays artifacts from every era of history pertaining to Jerusalem and the Holy Land. The most interesting building in the museum complex is the Shrine of the Book, which was built to house the famous Dead Sea Scrolls. These scrolls were found in a cave near the Dead Sea by a shepherd in 1947, packed in ancient pottery jars. They are the oldest existing fragments of the biblical scriptures ever found. The scrolls themselves are displayed in a case that was built to resemble the wooden rods around which the Jewish Torah scrolls

nians. Jews were not permitted to visit the Western Wall or the Mount of Olives, where many Jewish cemeteries are located. Sixty synagogues, many of them ancient and magnificent buildings such as the Hurva Synagogue, were destroyed, and their Torah scrolls, sacred scriptures to the Jews, were burned. The cemeteries on the Mount of Olives were vandalized, as thousands of graves were dug up and the bones scattered. Tombstones were smashed or used to build houses and pave roads.

In the early twentieth century, similar desecrations took place when Muslims were told to protect the Haram al-Sharif from being taken over by the Jews. They smeared the Western Wall with excrement, brought their flocks there to litter the area with manure, and used it as a garbage dump. Some of the Arab homes in the neighborhood were built right up against the wall, and some of the toilets actually leaned against it.

All of these desecrations can be compared historically to the Roman creation of Aelia Capitolina, when pagan temples were built on top of many sacred Jewish sites, and the Ottoman period, when Christian holy sites were destroyed or reconsecrated as Muslim holy places. History in Jerusalem continues to repeat itself over thousands of years.

are rolled for readings at synagogue services. The shrine, with its ceramic tiled dome, was constructed to look like the earthenware lid that covered the pottery jars in which the scrolls were found.

The Rockefeller Museum, also in West Jerusalem, is now part of the Israel Museum. It was founded in 1927 through a gift from U.S. financier John D. Rockefeller, and for many years housed the best collection of Holy Land artifacts in the Middle East. It was built with white Jerusalem limestone and looks like a Spanish castle with a central courtyard.

The Knesset

Israel's parliament building, the Knesset, is a simple cube-shaped building unlike the huge ornate buildings of government

An interior view of the Israel Museum, where the Dead Sea Scrolls are enshrined.

in many other countries. The parliament consists of 120 members, based on the same number of men who governed Jerusalem in the time of Herod's Second Temple. The Knesset was built in 1966 and was designed to incorporate classical elements of architecture from the Greeks as well as columns and a flat roof similar to what Herod's Second Temple is believed to have looked like. The reception area inside has stained glass windows designed by the Russian-Jewish artist Marc Chagall, as well as his mosaic floors and wall tapestries. Outside the Knesset stands a huge seven-branched menorah, the Jewish candelabra that is used as a symbol of Israel. The menorah was a gift from the British Parliament and is decorated with sculptures that represent different moments in Jewish history. Near the monument is an eternal flame that commemorates the Jews killed in the Holocaust and the Israeli wars.

THE HOLOCAUST MUSEUM

Yad Vashem, the Holocaust Museum in West Jerusalem, is an archive, museum, monument, and research center for everything pertaining to the Holocaust of World War II, when more than 6 million Jews were systematically murdered in Nazi concentration camps around Europe. The entrance to the museum is along the Avenue of the Righteous Among Nations, with plaques that show the names of those who put their own lives at risk to help the Jews. Inside the museum is the Hall of Remembrance, a stark room with the names of the twenty-one Nazi death camps engraved on flat black slabs, and a casket of ashes from one of the camp crematoriums in the center of the room. There are more than twenty monuments within the hillside site of the museum, and most modern tourists to Jerusalem find it is the most moving experience of their visit.

Across the street from Yad Vashem is a Protestant cemetery with the grave of Oskar Schindler, one of the most famous gentiles who helped to save Jews during the Holocaust. By employing twelve hundred Jews in his factory, Schindler saved them from the concentration camps. He is best known as the subject of Steven Spielberg's movie *Schindler's List*. After his death he was brought to Israel for burial through the efforts of some of the Jews he had rescued.

THE KENNEDY MEMORIAL

One other memorial found outside of Jerusalem is especially important to Americans. Located within the Jerusalem Forest, the Kennedy Memorial, or Yad Kennedy, honors American president John F. Kennedy and was built in 1966, three years after his assassination. The sixty-foot-high monument was designed to look like a tree stump, symbolizing a life cut short. The monument stands on a mountaintop and is encircled by fifty-one columns, each one bearing the name of one of the fifty United States and the District of Columbia.

Israelis traditionally honor someone's memory by planting a tree, and in August 1999, after the death of President Kennedy's son, John F. Kennedy Jr., and Kennedy Jr.'s wife in a plane crash, trees were planted in their honor near the Kennedy Memorial.

BUILDING JERUSALEM'S FUTURE

Like any modern city, Jerusalem is continuing to build and expand, despite the potential unrest in the area. And like many other cities, building styles and urban planning designs constantly evolve. These new projects will give Jerusalem an even more varied and distinctive look, as architect David Kroyanker describes:

The striking Hall of Remembrance is located in Yad Vashem, the Holocaust Museum in West Jerusalem.

Numerous construction projects are currently underway in Jerusalem. When they are completed, the shape of the city will be significantly altered. The most dramatic changes, it seems, will take place in the Jerusalem skyline. New twenty- and thirty-story buildings, so far considered "impossible" to build in Jerusalem, will appear. Glass walls—as opposed to stone—will become more frequent.[16]

As with any city, Jerusalem will be constantly changing, both to suit the needs and tastes of modern life, and as a result of political issues that continually spawn violence and destruction.

THE STRUGGLE FOR THE TEMPLE MOUNT

One of the greatest challenges facing Israel and the city of Jerusalem is the continued political strife taking place daily in the Middle East. The conflict between the Israelis and the Palestinians over the rightful ownership of the city and its many sacred sites constantly erupts into violence that exacts a high price in human lives and damage to Jerusalem itself. The newest threats to the city and its historic buildings stem from the continued struggle over the ownership of the Temple Mount. The Muslims claim the Dome of the Rock and the Haram al-Sharif on top of the Mount, and feel that this claim extends to the area beneath these monuments as well. The Jewish people claim the sacred Wailing Wall and also feel that they should be permitted to explore and possibly excavate the area that once lay beneath the Second Temple, for clues about the Temple of Solomon and what it may reveal about ancient life in Jerusalem.

Israelis are now protesting what they consider to be illegal excavations being carried out on the Temple Mount as the Muslims construct new stairways and entrances to the Haram al-Sharif and a new prayer hall beneath in the area once called Solomon's Stables:

> In 1996, Ramadan [a Muslim holy month, marked by daily fasting] fell during the coldest, rainiest days of the raw Jerusalem winter. The Waqf [Muslim] authorities reportedly received a quiet OK from the . . . government to use the underground vaults known as Solomon's Stables as a prayer hall. Within a year, the temporary shelter became permanent. The Al-Aksa Association raised money for building materials. . . . Bad weather wasn't the only reason for developing the space. Says Ahmad Agbariya [leader of the Al-Aksa Association]: "Information reached us that Jews wanted to take it for a synagogue."[17]

The Muslims have continued to excavate areas on the Temple Mount to meet their ever-increasing need for worship space. This continues to raise controversy about the possible destruction of historic material.

> In the last November of the Millennium, bulldozers arrived on the Mount. Over the next two months, they chewed out a thirty-foot-deep triangular pit: a long slope for steps, a vertical stone wall showing the arched vaults of Solomon's Stables. Two arches would become a wide entrance. In the cross-section on one side of the pit, the round bases of a half dozen stone columns, debris of an

unknown period, could be seen. A horizontal row of stones testified, perhaps, to a forgotten floor or ceiling, sliced by the earthmovers.[18]

The Jewish people are especially concerned about the earth that has been excavated from the Temple Mount and the possible destruction of layers of archaeological strata, which may contain important portions of Herod's Second Temple and possibly even Solomon's First Temple. They have formed the Committee to Prevent the Destruction of Antiquities on the Temple Mount. They feel that layers of earth containing important archaeological data have been removed and dumped, and proper archaeological supervision was never provided. This committee claims that tests conducted at this dump site have revealed shards and evidence from all eras of Jerusalem's history.

In 1996, controversy over the Temple Mount sparked a conflict known as the Tunnel War, in which Muslims and Jews fought once again over the sacred ground on and beneath Jerusalem's Temple Mount. In September 1996, the mayor of Jerusalem, Ehud Olmert, went into the Old City in the middle of the night with a band of soldiers and opened up a back entrance to the tunnel that runs along the base of the Wailing Wall. This new exit opened onto the Via Dolorosa, and completed a tourist route that led past thousands of years of Jerusalem history, from foundation stones of Herod's era to Roman streets to crusader churches to the present day.

The Muslims interpreted this new tunnel entrance as a desecration of the Dome of the Rock. The incident sparked a protest that quickly turned into fighting, as Israelis and Palestinians shot at each other throughout Jerusalem and the surrounding areas, killing seventy-five people.

BUILDING A THIRD TEMPLE

There have also been episodes with Jewish groups who believe that a third temple should be built on the site of the previous two Jewish temples on the Temple Mount. This adds further conflict between Muslims and Jews over who really holds the rights to the sacred area. In October 1990, a group called the Temple Mount Faithful announced that they intended to lay a symbolic cornerstone for the third temple:

An Israeli soldier pelted by a hail of stones attempts to escape Palestinian attackers near St. Stephen's Gate, Jerusalem.

The police initially told the Jewish group that they would be permitted to enter the Mount in pairs with a police escort. Violence ensued when Arabs began throwing stones and bottles at the police, some of which landed on Jews praying at the Western Wall. Nobody was seriously hurt but police and soldiers responded with disproportionate force. Twenty-one Arabs were killed, several shot in the back, and more than 100 wounded during clashes on the Haram with Israeli security forces. It was the largest death toll on a single day in the course of the intifada and its location was a huge symbolic provocation to all Muslims.[19]

Other groups have also made plans for a third temple, many of them using modern technology such as ultrasound imaging to prove the location of the first temples and lay claim to the ground of the Temple Mount. Others have set out to show that the historic temples were actually located in areas of the Mount far from the Dome of the Rock and the Al-Aksa Mosque, and that the Jewish people should be able to construct a temple that will coexist with the Muslims' holy sites.

In December 2000, President Bill Clinton of the United States presented his own idea for solving the question of who should control the Temple Mount in Jerusalem. He suggested: "[This proposal will maintain] Palestine sovereignty over the Haram [al-Sharif] and Israeli sovereignty over the Western Wall and shared functional sovereignty over the issue of excavation under the Haram and behind the Wall such that mutual consent

ARCHAEOLOGY IN THE HOLY LAND

Another source of conflict within Jerusalem often surrounds the various archaeological expeditions that take place in the Holy Land every year. Not only is there conflict over what group digs where, such as Christian groups who want to dig near the grounds of the Haram al-Sharif, but there are also issues such as the safety of these groups in the political climate of Israel, as well as differences in belief as to the handling of ancient remains.

Biblical Archaeology Review magazine publishes a monthly update on archaeological digs taking place in the Holy Land, and at times of severe unrest in the area, many such digs, which are often staffed with large numbers of U.S. volunteers, do not take place. Only those that are carried out well away from the modern cities and politically contested areas are considered to be safe.

Archaeology will continue to be an important issue in Jerusalem. As the city expands and more construction is carried out, workers will still find ancient remains of buildings and perhaps people, and decisions must be made as to who will explore and catalog these findings. Groups will continue to disagree with each other as to the importance of various sites, as in the conflict over the Muslim digging underground at the Dome of the Rock and the outcry by Jews who see it as the destruction of vital archaeological data. It is an issue firmly tied to the ownership questions that plague all parts of Jerusalem.

Without a resolution of the religious and political conflicts that have plagued Jerusalem for centuries, the welfare of both the city and its people remains at risk.

would be requested before any excavation can take place."[20] Although both sides were somewhat positive about President Clinton's proposal, the question of ownership still persists. The struggle has even reached cyberspace, since both Jewish and Muslim factions compete on the Internet with websites dedicated to their claims of the Temple Mount.

Another threat to the peaceful coexistence between Jews and Muslims in Jerusalem concerns a bulge that has appeared in one of the original stone walls of the Temple Mount, protruding more than two feet and putting the wall at risk of collapsing. Possible reasons for the bulge are poor maintenance and erosion, as well as the underground construction being carried out by the Muslims. The real danger is that a collapse of the wall could spark yet another conflict, with the Jews blaming the Muslims for the collapse and the Muslims blaming the Jews because of excavations that took place outside the wall in the decade after 1967.

The future of Jerusalem is just as uncertain as it has been throughout its long and violent history. Wars and strife take a heavy toll on the historic buildings of the city, and in the modern age of suicide bombers and car bombs, none of the city's most sacred buildings are safe from damage or destruction.

NOTES

Introduction
1. Quoted in Meron Benvenisti, *City of Stone: The Hidden History of Jerusalem*. Berkeley: University of California Press, 1996, p. 1.

Chapter 1: King Herod's Jerusalem
2. Teddy Kollek and Moshe Pearlman, *Jerusalem: A History of Forty Centuries*. New York: Random House, 1968, p. 100.
3. Agency for Jewish Education, "Jerusalem 3000: The Kotel," 1996. www.amyisrael.co.il.
4. Gershom Gorenberg, *The End of Days*. New York: Oxford University Press, 2002, p. 102.
5. Quoted in Agency for Jewish Education, "Jerusalem 3000."

Chapter 2: Roman Jerusalem
6. Quoted in William Whiston, *The Works of Josephus*. Peabody, MA: Hendrickson Publishers, 2001, p. 727.
7. Quoted in Whiston, *The Works of Josephus*, p. 741.
8. Quoted in Lambert Dolphin, "The Destruction of the Second Temple," 1996. www.templemount.org.
9. Quoted in State of Israel, "Jerusalem: The Northern Gate of Aelia Capitolina," 1999. www.israel.org.

Chapter 3: Muslim Jerusalem
10. Quoted in Jerry M. Landay, *Dome of the Rock*. New York: Newsweek Books, 1972, p. 71.
11. Gorenberg, *The End of Days*, p. 108.

Chapter 4: Christian Jerusalem
12. Quoted in Elizabeth Hallam, ed., *Chronicles of the Crusades: Eyewitness Accounts of the Wars Between Christianity and Islam*. New York: Salamander Books, 2000, p. 25.
13. Quoted in Hallam, *Chronicles of the Crusades*, p. 89.
14. Quoted In Hallam, *Chronicles of the Crusades*, p. 93.

Chapter 5: Modern Jerusalem
15. Bernard Wasserstein, *Divided Jerusalem*. New Haven, CT: Yale University Press, 2001, p. 217.

16. David Kroyanker, "Fifty Years of Israeli Architecture as Reflected in Jerusalem's Buildings," 1999. www.mfa.gov.

17. Gorenberg, *The End of Days*, p. 198.

18. Gorenberg, *The End of Days*, p. 200.

19. Wasserstein, *Divided Jerusalem*, p. 337.

20. Quoted in Wasserstein, *Divided Jerusalem*, pp. 348–49.

GLOSSARY

adzes: Heavy curved tools for shaping timbers or stone.

Aelia Capitolina: The name given to the Roman city built over the ruins of Jerusalem after A.D. 70.

Al-Aksa Mosque: The Muslim place of worship built near the Dome of the Rock, on Jerusalem's Temple Mount.

aqueduct: An artificial channel for conducting water over long distances.

basilica: A large oblong Roman building used as a hall of justice and public meeting place.

battlement: A defensive wall on the roof of a castle or fortress, often notched at regular intervals to allow for firing weapons.

brocade: A type of fabric woven with a raised overall pattern.

caliph: A spiritual leader of the Islamic religion, who can claim to be a direct descendent of Muhammad.

cardo: The main north-south street of an ancient Roman city.

castrum: A Roman military camp, usually square or rectangular in shape.

Church of the Holy Sepulchre: The Jerusalem church built over the traditional sites of Jesus Christ's death and burial.

Dome of the Rock: The Muslim shrine built over the sacred rock of Muhammad on Jerusalem's Temple Mount.

Edicule: The small monument built around Jesus Christ's tomb within the Church of the Holy Sepulchre.

forum: The marketplace or public square of an ancient Roman city.

garrison: A military post or fortified area, occupied by troops.

gild: To coat something with gold, gold leaf, or a gold-colored substance.

Haram al-Sharif: Translated as "the Noble Sanctuary," this is the Muslim name given to Jerusalem's Temple Mount.

hippodrome: An ancient Roman arena used for horse and chariot racing.

master course: The first row of stones placed when building a wall or structure.

minaret: A slender tower attached to a mosque, from which people are called to prayer.

mortar: A mixture of lime or cement, sand, and water, used to bond bricks and stones together.

mosaic: A picture or decoration made of small pieces of inlaid stone or glass.

patron: A person who supports another person, activity, or organization with money or effort.

quarrying: Excavating stone from the ground by cutting or blasting.

rotunda: A round building or hall topped by a dome.

shrine: A structure or place that is considered to be holy because of its religious or historical association.

synagogue: A Jewish place of worship.

turret: A small tower, usually forming part of a larger structure such as a castle or fortress.

Wailing Wall: The Western Wall of Herod's original Second Temple in Jerusalem, where Jews gather together for prayer or expressions of grief.

FOR FURTHER READING

Michael and Caroline Carroll, *Exploring Ancient Cities of the Bible*. Colorado Springs, CO: Cook Communications Ministries, 2001. An illustrated guide to the history and archaeology of ancient biblical cities.

Robert Green, *Herod the Great*. New York: Franklin Watts, 1996. King Herod's life, including his building projects throughout the Holy Land.

David Macaulay, *City: A Story of Roman Planning and Construction*. New York: Houghton Mifflin, 1974. The complete story of the process of constructing a Roman city, with excellent illustrations.

Saviour Pirotta, *Holy Cities: Jerusalem*. New York: Dillon Press, 1993. An illustrated history of Jerusalem, including an overview of modern life in the city.

Melanie Rice, Christopher Rice, and Christopher Gravett, *Crusades: The Struggle for the Holy Lands*. New York: Dorling Kindersley, 2001. An illustrated history of all the crusades to the Holy Land.

Max Schwartz, *Machines, Buildings, Weaponry of Biblical Times*. Old Tappan, NJ: Fleming H. Revell, 1990. Excellent explanations of how buildings and machinery were constructed and used in biblical times.

Diane Slavik, *Daily Life in Ancient and Modern Jerusalem*. Minneapolis: Lerner Publishing, 2001. Daily life throughout the history of Jerusalem, from King David to the present day.

Time-Life Books, *Lost Civilizations: The Holy Land*. Alexandria, VA: Time-Life Books, 1992. A overview of ancient civilizations in the Holy Land.

Jonathan N. Tubb, *Eyewitness Books: Bible Lands*. New York: Dorling Kindersley, 2000. An exploration of the lands of the Bible, including photographs of places and artifacts.

WORKS CONSULTED

BOOKS

Lesley and Roy A. Adkins, *Handbook to Life in Ancient Rome.* New York: Oxford University Press, 1994. An excellent reference about every aspect of Roman life.

Elkan Nathan Adler, *Jewish Travellers in the Middle Ages.* New York: Dover Publications, 1987. Firsthand accounts of Jewish travelers in the ninth to fifteenth centuries.

Kamil J. Asali, ed., *Jerusalem in History: 3000 B.C. to the Present Day.* London: Kegan Paul International, 1997. A detailed and objective overview of Jerusalem's history.

Graeme Auld and Margreet Steiner, *Jerusalem I: From the Bronze Age to the Maccabees.* Macon, GA: Mercer University Press, 1996. An archaeologically based history of early Jerusalem.

James Turner Barclay, *The City of the Great King.* Philadelphia: Arno Press, 1977. Barclay's story of his visit to Jerusalem in the early nineteenth century.

Meron Benvenisti, *City of Stone: The Hidden History of Jerusalem.* Berkeley: University of California Press, 1996. A historical look at the city written by a former deputy mayor.

Martin Biddle, *The Tomb of Christ.* Gloucestershire, UK: Sutton Publishing, 1999. An in-depth study of Jesus' tomb and the Church of the Holy Sepulchre.

John Dominic Crossan and Jonathan L. Reed, *Excavating Jesus: Beneath the Stones, Behind the Texts.* San Francisco: HarperCollins, 2001. A study of biblical history as it can be verified through archaeology.

Dorling Kindersley Travel Guides, *Jerusalem and the Holy Land.* New York: Dorling Kindersley, 2000. A complete travel guide to Jerusalem and the Holy Land.

Richard Ettinghausen and Oleg Grabar, *The Art and Architecture of Islam 650–1250*. New Haven, CT: Yale University Press, 1994. An overview of early Islamic art and architecture.

Brian M. Fagan, ed., *Eyewitness to Discovery*. New York: Oxford University Press, 1996. A fascinating collection of writings by archaeologists about famous discoveries.

John Fitchen, *Building Construction Before Mechanization*. Boston: MIT Press, 1999. A study of how buildings were constructed before the use of modern machinery.

Alec Garrard, *The Splendor of the Temple: A Pictorial Guide to Herod's Temple and Its Ceremonies*. Grand Rapids, MI: Kregel Publications, 2000. A thorough guide to King Herod's Temple, illustrated with photos of the author's temple model.

Gershom Gorenberg, *The End of Days*. New York: Oxford University Press, 2002. Explores the struggle for control of the Temple Mount, especially in terms of modern Jerusalem.

Pierre Grimal, *Roman Cities*. Madison: University of Wisconsin Press, 1983. A comprehensive look at the structure of Roman cities all over the world.

Elizabeth Hallam, ed., *Chronicles of the Crusades: Eyewitness Accounts of the Wars Between Christianity and Islam*. New York: Salamander Books, 2000. A collection of narratives by actual witnesses to the Crusades.

Roberta L. Harris, *The World of the Bible*. New York: Thames and Hudson, 1995. An illustrated guide to biblical history and places from a Christian perspective.

Thomas A. Idinopulos, *Jerusalem*. Chicago: Ivan R. Dee, 1991. Jerusalem's history as seen through the struggles of three religions.

Daniel Jacobs, *Jerusalem Mini-Rough Guide*. New York: Penguin Books, 1999. A modern travel guide to Jerusalem's sights.

Teddy Kollek and Moshe Pearlman, *Jerusalem: A History of Forty Centuries*. New York: Random House, 1968. An excellent history of Jerusalem written by its former mayor.

Jerry M. Landay, *Dome of the Rock*. New York: Newsweek Books, 1972. A history of the Dome of the Rock, including its construction.

Magnus Magnusson, *BC: The Archaeology of the Bible Lands*. London: The Bodley Head and BBC, 1977. Biblical history through an archaeological perspective.

Amy Dockser Marcus, *The View from Nebo: How Archaeology Is Rewriting the Bible and Reshaping the Middle East*. Boston: Little, Brown, 2000. How modern archaeology is affecting established views of biblical history.

Jerome Murphy-O'Connor, *Oxford Archaeological Guides: The Holy Land*. New York: Oxford University Press, 1998. An archaeologically based travel guide to the Holy Land.

New York Times Correspondents, *Israel: The Historical Atlas From Ancient Times to the Modern Nation*. New York: Macmillan Publishing, 1997. A primarily modern look at Israel through news articles in the *New York Times*.

Alan Paris, *Jerusalem 3000: Kids Discover the City of Gold*. New York: Pitspopany Press, 1995. A quick overview of Jerusalem's history from a Jewish perspective.

Jonathan Riley-Smith, *The Oxford Illustrated History of the Crusades*. New York: Oxford University Press, 1995. A detailed history of the Crusades.

Hershel Shanks, *Ancient Israel: From Abraham to the Roman Destruction of the Temple*. Washington, DC: Biblical Archaeology Society, 1999. A history of early Jerusalem.

Daniel Sperber, *The City in Roman Palestine*. New York: Oxford University Press, 1998. A specific history of Roman cities in the Holy Land.

John Lloyd Stephens, *Incidents of Travel in Egypt, Arabia Petraea, and the Holy Land*. New York: Dover Publications, 1996. Stephens's accounts of his travels in the early 1800s.

Carsten Peter Thiede and Matthew d'Ancona, *The Quest for the True Cross*. New York: Palgrave, 2000. An exploration of the discovery of Jesus' cross and its authenticity.

Colin Thubron, *Great Cities: Jerusalem*. Amsterdam: Time-Life International, 1976. An illustrated look at twentieth-century Jerusalem.

Bernard Wasserstein, *Divided Jerusalem: The Struggle for the Holy City*. New Haven, CT: Yale University Press, 2001. A complete history of the struggles between three religions and their claims on Jerusalem.

William Whiston, *The Works of Josephus*. Peabody, MA: Hendrickson Publishers, 2001. The collected works of the ancient Roman historian Josephus.

PERIODICALS

David Jacobson, "Herod's Roman Temple," *Biblical Archaeology Review*, March/April 2002.

Kathleen Ritmeyer and Leen Ritmeyer, "Jerusalem's Russian Compound," *Biblical Archaeology Review*, January/February 2002.

Hershel Shanks, "Temple Mount Wall in Danger," *Biblical Archaeology Review*, January/February 2002.

INTERNET SOURCES

Agency for Jewish Education, "Jerusalem 3000: The Kotel," 1996. www.amyisrael.co.il. An excellent website for historical information about Jerusalem.

Ancient Sandals, "Tour of Jerusalem and the Holy Land," 2001. www.ancientsandals.com. Photographic tours of Holy Land sights.

Lambert Dolphin, "The Destruction of the Second Temple," 1996. www.templemount.org. A complete description of the Roman destruction of the Second Temple.

Holyland Hotel, "Virtual Tour of Temple Model," 2001. www.inisrael.com. Virtual tour of the model of Herod's Jerusalem on the grounds of the Holyland Hotel in Jerusalem.

Israel Ministry of Foreign Affairs, "Archaeological Sites," 2002. www.israel-mfa.gov. Excellent archaeological information as well as current news and events in the city.

———, David Kroyanker, "Fifty Years of Israeli Architecture as reflected in Jerusalem's Buildings," 1999. www.mfa.gov.

State of Israel, "Jerusalem: The Northern Gate of Aelia Capitolina," 1999. www.israel.org.

INDEX

Picture Credits

Cover Images: (clockwise from top) © Richard T. Nowitz/CORBIS, © Hulton Archive by Getty Images, The Art Archive/San Angelo in Formis Capua Italy/Dagli Orti.

© Archivo Iconografico, S.A./CORBIS 32

Associated Press 14, 25, 87

© Bettmann/CORBIS 41, 66

© Dean Conger/CORBIS 49

© Corel Corporation 12, 27, 35, 52, 56, 72, 82

© Historical Picture Archive/CORBIS 30

Hulton/Archive by Getty Images 21, 44, 55, 60, 64, 71, 80

© Hanan Isachar/CORBIS 69

© Charles and Josette Lenars/CORBIS 40

© James Marshall/CORBIS 78

© Michael Maslan Historic Photographs/CORBIS 46

© Carmen Redondo/CORBIS 18, 38

© David Rubinger/CORBIS 84

© Ted Spiegel/CORBIS 89

About the Author

Marcia Amidon Lüsted has a degree in English and secondary education, and has worked as a middle school English teacher, a musician, and a bookseller. She lives in New Hampshire with her husband, three sons, and two cats, and in her spare time enjoys reading, writing, history, traveling, and playing the piano.